FORWARD/COMMENTARY

The National Institute of Standards and Technology (NIST) is a measurement standards laboratory, and a non-regulatory agency of the **United States Department of Commerce**. Its mission is to promote innovation and industrial competitiveness. Founded in 1901, as the National Bureau of Standards, NIST was formed with the mandate to provide standard weights and measures, and to serve as the national physical laboratory for the United States. **With a** world-class measurement and testing laboratory encompassing a wide range of areas of computer science, mathematics, statistics, and systems engineering, NIST's cybersecurity program supports its overall mission to promote U.S. innovation and industrial competitiveness by advancing measurement science, standards, and related technology through research and development in ways that enhance economic security and improve our quality of life.

The need for cybersecurity standards and best practices that address interoperability, usability and privacy has been shown to be critical for the nation. NIST's cybersecurity programs seek to enable greater development and application of practical, innovative security technologies and methodologies that enhance the country's ability to address current and future computer and information security challenges.

The cybersecurity publications produced by NIST cover a wide range of cybersecurity concepts that are carefully designed to work together to produce a holistic approach to cybersecurity primarily for government agencies and constitute the best practices used by industry. This holistic strategy to cybersecurity covers the gamut of security subjects from development of secure encryption standards for communication and storage of information while at rest to how best to recover from a cyber-attack.

Why buy a book you can download for free?   We print this so you don't have to.

Some are available only in electronic media. Some online docs are missing pages or barely legible.

We at 4th Watch Publishing are former government employees, so we know how government employees actually use the standards. When a new standard is released, an engineer prints it out, punches holes and puts it in a 3-ring binder. While this is not a big deal for a 5 or 10-page document, many NIST documents are over 100 pages and printing a large document is a time-consuming effort. So, an engineer that's paid $75 an hour is spending hours simply printing out the tools needed to do the job. That's time that could be better spent doing engineering. We publish these documents so engineers can focus on what they were hired to do – engineering. It's much more cost-effective to just order the latest version from Amazon.com

If there is a standard you would like published, let us know. Our web site is usgovpub.com

NIST Technical Note 2051

Cybersecurity Framework Smart Grid Profile

This publication is available free of charge from:
https://doi.org/10.6028/NIST.TN.2051

National Institute of
Standards and Technology
U.S. Department of Commerce

NIST Technical Note 2051

Cybersecurity Framework Smart Grid Profile

Jeffrey Marron
Applied Cybersecurity Division
Information Technology Laboratory

Avi Gopstein
Office of Smart Grid and Cyber-Physical Systems
Engineering Laboratory

Nadya Bartol
Boston Consulting Group
Bethesda, MD

Valery Feldman
HII Mission Driven Innovative Solutions (HII-MDIS)
Annapolis Junction, MD

This publication is available free of charge from:
https://doi.org/10.6028/NIST.TN.2051

July 2019

U.S. Department of Commerce
Wilbur L. Ross, Jr., Secretary

National Institute of Standards and Technology
Walter Copan, NIST Director and Undersecretary of Commerce for Standards and Technology

National Institute of Standards and Technology Technical Note 2051
Natl. Inst. Stand. Technol. Tech. Note 2051, 142 pages (July 2019)
CODEN: NTNOEF

This publication is available free of charge from:
https://doi.org/10.6028/NIST.TN.2051

Abstract

The Smart Grid Profile applies risk management strategies from the Framework for Improving Critical Infrastructure Cybersecurity (Cybersecurity Framework) to the smart grid and will serve as a foundation for refinements to support new grid architectures. The Profile provides cybersecurity risk management guidance to power system owners/operators by prioritizing cybersecurity activities based on their effectiveness in helping power system owners/operators achieve common high-level business objectives for the smart grid. The Profile also provides a list of considerations relevant to the challenges power system owners/operators may experience as they implement these cybersecurity activities in infrastructures with high concentrations of distributed energy resources (DERs).

Key words

Architecture; business/mission objectives; cybersecurity; Cybersecurity Framework (CSF); distributed energy resource (DER); grid modernization; Pacific Northwest National Laboratory (PNNL); Profile; reliability; resilience; safety; smart grid.

Table of Contents

List of Tables

List of Figures

1. Executive Summary

The U.S. electric power grid is undergoing modernization to make the grid "smart." The smart grid utilizes intelligent and distributed technologies to make the power grid more reliable and resilient to disruptions. While there are clear benefits to this evolution, the modernization effort is not easy. Power system owners/operators[1] will face numerous challenges as they strive to modernize their own capabilities, while also interfacing and co-existing with other power system owners/operators at different stages of the modernization process. Along with the benefits of the smart grid, there are cybersecurity risks that need to be considered to ensure a safe, effective grid transformation.

The Smart Grid Profile applies risk management strategies from the Framework for Improving Critical Infrastructure Cybersecurity (Cybersecurity Framework, explained in Sec. 3) to the smart grid and will serve as a foundation for refinements to support new grid architectures. The Profile provides cybersecurity risk management guidance to power system owners/operators by prioritizing[2] cybersecurity activities based on their effectiveness in helping power system owners/operators achieve common high-level business objectives for the smart grid. These high-level business objectives are:

- Maintain safety

- Maintain power system reliability

- Maintain power system resilience

- Support grid modernization

The Profile also provides power system owners/operators with considerations[3] relevant to the challenges they may experience as they implement these cybersecurity activities in infrastructures with high concentrations of distributed energy resources (DERs).

The following are some examples of how power system owners/operators may use the Smart Grid Profile:

- Prioritizing organizational cybersecurity activities to align with available resources

- Enabling better informed decision making about cybersecurity activities by referencing the considerations listed for each cybersecurity activity

- Conveying cybersecurity requirements to an external entity such as a service provider

- Gauging their organizational cybersecurity posture against the prioritized cybersecurity activities

In smart grid environments, power system owners/operators rely on and interact with a larger community of diverse third parties than in traditional grid environments. These third parties

---

[1] In this Profile, "power system owners/operators" refers primarily to distribution grid owners rather than customers and the assets that they own "behind the meter."
[2] The prioritization of cybersecurity activities in this Profile consists of a binary "yes/no" determinations and is discussed in more detail in Sec. 4
[3] A consideration is an interest in something relevant to one or more stakeholders. Considerations cover both things that are of interest for positive or negative reasons. Considerations should be used to drive requirements. See Sec. 4 for more information about the use of considerations in this Profile.

include but are not limited to vendors, suppliers, contractors, distributed generation owners/operators, and consumers. Many of the cybersecurity activities that power system owners/operators traditionally implemented within their own infrastructures will need to be extended to the third party-owned devices and infrastructures that interconnect with the power system infrastructure. Furthermore, supply chain risk management considerations are relevant in these relationships especially when smart grid devices and systems are interconnecting with third parties. In addition to using the Cybersecurity Framework to help assess and manage risks associated with third parties, power systems owners/operators may consult Cybersecurity Procurement Language for Energy Delivery Systems [10] and Utilities Telecom Council (UTC) white paper [11] for more specific guidance.

Notes to Readers:

The smart grid is a complex system composed of a large community of diverse parties, each with varied interests and perspectives. This Profile is focused on cybersecurity needs of smart grid owners/operators and therefore may not be sufficiently useful by itself to all the diverse parties in the smart grid.

The Profile indicates those cybersecurity activities which can directly help power system owners/operators achieve high-level business objectives. However, the Profile's greatest value may be the description of considerations[3] that power system owners/operators may have to address as they implement the cybersecurity activities. The Profile can also help owners/operators evaluate how the responsibilities for these considerations change as they modernize equipment and as actors take on new roles within the power system.

2. Importance of Cybersecurity in the Smart Grid

The U.S. electric power grid has provided inexpensive, reliable power for decades. Even as electric utilities incorporate new technologies and accommodate changing customer expectations, the basic structure of the grid remains broadly consistent with the first electric systems build more than a century ago. In the traditional grid, power flows in one direction— from centralized generation facilities, through transmission lines, and to customers via distribution utilities. The centralized design has historically brought efficiencies in facilities and operations but has also made the grid vulnerable to both malicious actions and natural disasters. Also new technologies and operational solutions—and their unique vulnerabilities—are becoming more important as evolving demands from economic development to diversifying customer expectations come in conflict with the physical constraints of decades old infrastructure.

The U.S. electric power grid is undergoing modernization to make the grid "smart." In contrast to the traditional grid, a smart grid features intelligent and distributed technologies such as advanced metering infrastructure (AMI) and automated distribution management systems that will enable the grid to incorporate new technologies and resources. By enhancing data utilization at the grid-edge to accommodate bi-directional power flows and other system dynamics inherent to extensive adoption of distributed energy resources (DERs), the grid will become more resilient to disruptions and resilient in the face of attack [3]. As observability and control extend to the grid-edge, customers and other participants will see new economic opportunities through access to wholesale and other energy markets. However, these opportunities carry obligations not previously assigned to customers to support the overall cyber and operational health of the grid.

While the benefits of the smart grid are clear, it will not be an easy modernization effort. Transitioning to the future grid has been compared to the building of the interstate highway system [3]. In the same way that the interstate highway system took decades to complete, modernization of the grid will take coordinated planning and execution that evolves over time. There will be milestones in which the grid will become "smarter," but the full realization of the smart grid will take a decade or more. Along the way, there will be challenges for power system owners/operators as they both strive to modernize their own capabilities while interfacing and co-existing with other power system owners/operators that are at different stages of the transformation process. The fact that the grid is already in use and pervasive in modern society, and cannot be taken offline for this modernization effort, increases the complexity of these challenges.

The modernized grid will consist of a variety of different architectures.[4] Describing such architectures to guide technology implementation is important when planning for an effort as vast as grid modernization. Grid architectures—using the concepts of system architecture, network theory, and control theory—define the components, structure, behavior, qualities, properties, interactions, and limits of the electric power grid. As a high-level description of a grid, architectures provide several benefits: they help simplify complex grid interactions to understand and reduce risk; provide a shared vision of the future grid; and identify barriers to

---

[4] As a high-level description of a grid, architectures define the components, structure, behavior, qualities, properties, and limits of the electric power grid. This Profile explores a High-DER smart grid architecture developed by the Department of Energy's Pacific Northwest National Laboratory (PNNL). PNNL is developing other architectures to express different structural approaches to the smart grid

achieving that vision. The Department of Energy's (DoE) Pacific Northwest National Laboratory (PNNL) is one group developing high-level architectures of the smart grid. These architectures describe some of the stages along the grid transformation—from the near-term modernization that still relies on a conventional grid backbone to end states involving extensive automation and high-penetrations of DERs.

Despite the considerable benefits of the future grid, many aspects of the smart grid have cybersecurity risks that need to be considered to ensure a safe, effective grid transformation. The modern grid should be safe, reliable and resilient. A resilient grid has to be able to withstand not just hazards, human errors, hardware failure, and software bugs, but also cyber events as well. This document explores evolving grid architectures—including the high DER penetration architecture described by PNNL—and provides guidance for power system owners/operators to manage cybersecurity risks. To that end, the document draws heavily from the NIST Framework for Improving Critical Infrastructure Cybersecurity (Cybersecurity Framework, discussed in Sec. 3 below), helping power system owners/operators prioritize those cybersecurity activities that most align with power system goals of safety, reliability, resilience, and grid modernization. The document also provides considerations relevant to the challenges that power system owners/operators may face when implementing the cybersecurity activities.

3. Overview of the Cybersecurity Framework

Recognizing the national and economic security of the United States depends on the reliable functioning of critical infrastructure, the President issued Executive Order (EO) 13636, Improving Critical Infrastructure Cybersecurity, in February 2013. The EO directed NIST to work with stakeholders to develop a voluntary framework—based on existing standards, guidelines, and practices—for reducing cybersecurity risks to critical infrastructure.

Created through collaboration between industry and government, the Cybersecurity Framework seeks to promote the protection of critical infrastructure. The prioritized, flexible, and risk-based[5] approach of the Cybersecurity Framework helps owners and operators of critical infrastructure manage cybersecurity-related risk. Although it was designed for organization that are part of the U.S. critical infrastructure, many other organizations[6] in the private and public sectors (including federal agencies) are using the Cybersecurity Framework.

The Cybersecurity Framework consists of three main components: the Core[7], Implementation Tiers, and Profiles.

- The Framework Core provides a catalog of desired cybersecurity activities and outcomes[8] using common language. The Core guides organizations in managing and reducing their cybersecurity risks in a way that complements an organization's existing cybersecurity and risk management processes.

- The Framework Implementation Tiers provides context on how an organization views cybersecurity risk management. The Tiers help organizations understand whether they have a functioning and repeatable cybersecurity risk management process and the extent to which cybersecurity risk management is integrated with broader organizational risk management decisions.

- Framework Profiles are a customization of the outcomes of the Core to align with an organization's requirements. Profiles are primarily used to identify and prioritize opportunities for improving cybersecurity at an organization

The Core presents industry standards, guidelines, and practices within five concurrent and continuous Functions—Identify, Protect, Detect, Respond, and Recover. Each of these Functions is described below.

Identify – Develop the organizational understanding to manage cybersecurity risk to systems, assets, data, and capabilities. The activities in the Identify Function are foundational for effective

---

[5] Risk-based here is differentiated from a compliance-based approach to managing cybersecurity risk. A compliance-based approach often focuses on defining a set of requirements broadly applicable to all organizations. A risk-based approach recognizes that each organization has unique threats and risks and enables organizations to prioritize cybersecurity activities according to their environment, requirements, and budgetary considerations.

[6] This document uses the general word "organization" to show that the Cybersecurity Framework may be used by private businesses, government agencies, academia, etc.

[7] Elements of the Cybersecurity Framework—including Core, Implementation Tiers, Profile, Function, Category, and Subcategory—are normally capitalized and will be capitalized throughout this document

[8] The word "outcomes" is used because the Cybersecurity Framework focuses on the "what" not the "how." In other words, the emphasis is on the cybersecurity outcomes that the organization wants to achieve, but not how they will achieve it. The Informative References described on p. 7 help organizations with the "how."

use of the Cybersecurity Framework, enabling an organization to focus and prioritize its efforts, consistent with its risk management strategy and business needs.

Protect – Develop and implement the appropriate safeguards to ensure delivery of critical infrastructure services. The activities in the Protect Function support the ability to limit or contain the impact of a potential cybersecurity event.

Detect – Develop and implement the appropriate activities to identify the occurrence of a cybersecurity event. The activities in the Detect Function enable timely discovery of cybersecurity events.

Respond – Develop and implement the appropriate activities to take action regarding a detected cybersecurity event. The activities in the Respond Function support the ability to contain the impact of a potential cybersecurity event.

Recover – Develop and implement the appropriate activities to maintain plans for resilience and to restore any capabilities or services that were impaired due to a cybersecurity event. The activities in the Recover Function support timely recovery to normal operations to reduce the impact from a cybersecurity event.

When considered together, these Functions provide a high-level, strategic view of the lifecycle of an organization's management of cybersecurity risk. The Framework Core then identifies underlying Categories and Subcategories for each Function. The 108 Subcategories are the discrete cybersecurity outcomes that are organized into 23 Categories like "Asset Management" or "Supply Chain Risk Management." Table 1 shows the 5 Functions and 23 Categories of the Core.

Table 1 - Cybersecurity Framework Functions and Categories

Function Unique Identifier	Function	Category Unique Identifier	Category
ID	Identify		
			Supply Chain Risk Management
PR	Protect		
			Protective Technology
DE	Detect		
			Detection Processes
RS	Respond		
			Improvements
RC	Recover		
			Communications

Informative References—such as existing standards, guidelines, and practices—provide practical suggestions for how to achieve the desired outcome of each Subcategory. An example of two Subcategories, along with applicable Informative References, within the Supply Chain Risk Management Category is shown in **Table 2**.

Table 2 - Cybersecurity Framework Subcategory Examples

Function	Category	Subcategory	Informative References
Identify (ID)	**Supply Chain Risk Management (ID.SC):** The organization's priorities, constraints, risk tolerances, and assumptions are established and used to support risk decisions associated with managing supply chain risk. The organization has established and implemented the processes to identify, assess and manage supply chain risks.	**ID.SC-1**: Cyber supply chain risk management processes are identified, established, assessed, managed, and agreed to by organizational stakeholders	**CIS CSC** 4 **COBIT 5** APO10.01, APO10.04, APO12.04, APO12.05, APO13.02, BAI01.03, BAI02.03, BAI04.02 **ISA 62443-2-1:2009** 4.3.4.2 **ISO/IEC 27001:2013** A.15.1.1, A.15.1.2, A.15.1.3, A.15.2.1, A.15.2.2 **NIST SP 800-53 Rev. 4** SA-9, SA-12, PM-9
		ID.SC-2: Suppliers and third party partners of information systems, components, and services are identified, prioritized, and assessed using a cyber supply chain risk assessment process	**COBIT 5** APO10.01, APO10.02, APO10.04, APO10.05, APO12.01, APO12.02, APO12.03, APO12.04, APO12.05, APO12.06, APO13.02, BAI02.03 **ISA 62443-2-1:2009** 4.2.3.1, 4.2.3.2, 4.2.3.3, 4.2.3.4, 4.2.3.6, 4.2.3.8, 4.2.3.9, 4.2.3.10, 4.2.3.12, 4.2.3.13, 4.2.3.14 **ISO/IEC 27001:2013** A.15.2.1, A.15.2.2 **NIST SP 800-53 Rev. 4** RA-2, RA-3, SA-12, SA-14, SA-15, PM-9

Note that the Subcategory outcomes are organized according to Functions and Categories and are not prioritized within the Core. Each organization has unique requirements including risk tolerance and budget. Therefore, the prioritization of the Subcategory outcomes will vary from one organization to the next. This prioritization of Subcategory outcomes is the essence of a Profile.

One way to create a Profile is depicted in **Fig. 1**. In the center of the figure are the 108 cybersecurity Subcategory outcomes of the Core. As input to the evaluative process, an organization considers its high-level business objectives; any cybersecurity requirements through policy, legislation, and regulations; and any unique technical or environmental threats. The Subcategories which will best help the organization achieve its business objectives, meet cybersecurity requirements, and address technical and environmental threats are prioritized. For each prioritized Subcategory outcome, the Informative References of the Core can be used to identify specific technical guidance or controls catalogs that can help the organization achieve the cybersecurity outcome.

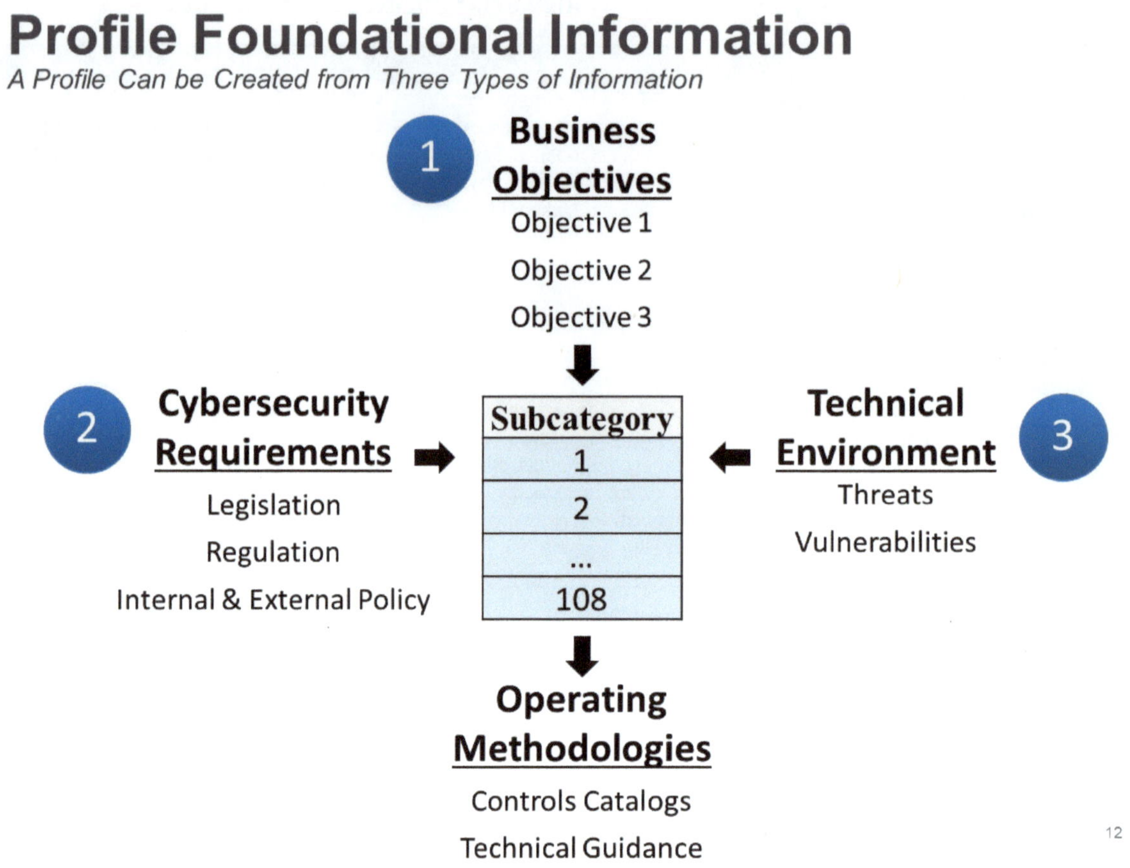

Profile Foundational Information

A Profile Can be Created from Three Types of Information

1 **Business Objectives**

Objective 1

Objective 2

Objective 3

⬇

2 **Cybersecurity Requirements** ➡

Legislation

Regulation

Internal & External Policy

Subcategory
1
2
...
108

⬅ **Technical Environment** **3**

Threats

Vulnerabilities

⬇

Operating Methodologies

Controls Catalogs

Technical Guidance

12

Fig. 1 - Cybersecurity Framework Profile Creation Process

Profiles can be created for individual organizations or even parts of an organization (e.g., organizational units such as Finance or Human Resources). Increasingly, however, Profiles are being created for entire critical infrastructure sectors (e.g., Financial Services sector) or for sub-sectors (e.g., Oil and Natural Gas sub-sector within the Energy sector). Since organizations within a sector or sub-sector share many of the same business objectives and regulatory requirements, creating high-level Profiles for the sector/sub-sector can provide a common starting prioritization of cybersecurity activities for all organizations within the sector/sub-sector. These Profiles can serve as a starting point, making it easier for organizations to begin incorporating cybersecurity and can also be used to provide a baseline of cybersecurity for organizations within a sector or sub-sector. Individual organizations can take the sector/sub-sector Profile and tailor it to address requirements, business objectives, or environmental threats unique to them.

4. Smart Grid Profile

The Smart Grid Profile is designed to be broadly applicable to power system owners/operators of an infrastructure composed of high penetrations of DER. It is intended to help power system owners/operators prioritize[9] cybersecurity activities based on high-level business objectives that are perceived as common throughout the smart grid. The Profile also presents considerations for power system owners/operators as they seek to achieve the outcome of each Subcategory. In addition to providing justifications for a Subcategory's selection, the considerations highlight challenges that power system owners/operators may encounter as they attempt to achieve the Subcategory outcomes. Figure 2 below, a snippet from the Profile, illustrates considerations for power system owners/operators for Subcategories ID.AM-1 *Physical devices and systems within the organization are inventoried* and ID.AM-2 *Software platforms and applications within the organization are inventoried*.

	Category	Maintain Safety	Maintain Reliability	Maintain Resilience	Support Grid Modernization	Considerations for Power System Owners/Operators
	Category	Subcategories				
ID	Asset Management	ID.AM-1	ID.AM-1	ID.AM-1	ID.AM-1	Knowing hardware assets is critical for maintaining safety, reliability, and resilience, as well as facilitating the transition to the modern grid. Legacy and modernized assets need to be known and understood. As modernized grids become more distributed, power system owners/operators need to be accountable for all distributed assets that they own.
		ID.AM-2	ID.AM-2	ID.AM-2	ID.AM-2	Knowing software assets is critical for maintaining reliability, and resilience, as well as facilitating the transition to the modern grid. Legacy and modernized assets need to be known and understood. This especially applies to modernized assets because the sophisticated logic that they execute is driven by software.

Fig. 2 - Example of Considerations for Power System Owners/Operators

While this Profile is based on a set of business objectives thought to be broadly applicable across the smart grid, individual power system owners/operators may need to tailor their selection of Subcategories. For example, a power system owner/operator may have additional business objectives or may be subject to state or local regulatory requirements not considered in this Profile. These requirements may impact the power system owner/operator's prioritization of Subcategory outcomes.

Development of this Smart Grid Profile consisted of the following steps:

1. Reviewed relevant literature, including available PNNL smart grid architecture documentation and NIST publications [4], [5], [6], [7].

2. Interviewed industry experts from power system owners/operators and electric power industry think tanks.

3. Developed a set of common business objectives based on the literature review and the interviews (discussed in greater detail in Sec. 5).

---

[9] The Subcategory prioritization in this document consists of a binary "yes/no" determination rather than a numerical prioritization (e.g., a rating scale from 1 to 5). Our intent is to identify those cybersecurity outcomes which will directly help power system owners/operators achieve the listed business objectives. More detailed prioritization of Subcategory outcomes will be highly dependent on each organization's unique risk tolerance, requirements, and budget constraints.

4.   Analyzed NIST Cybersecurity Framework v1.1 Framework Core Subcategories in relation to the identified business objectives. Identified which Subcategories directly assist power system owners/operators in achieving the business objectives identified in Sec. 5 of this document.

5.   For each Subcategory, described the rationale for its prioritization and/or composed relevant implementation considerations for power system owners/operators.

The following are some examples of how power system owners/operators may use the Smart Grid Profile:

- Prioritizing organizational cybersecurity activities to align with available resources.

- Enabling better informed decision making about cybersecurity activities by referencing the considerations listed for each Subcategory activity.

- Conveying cybersecurity requirements to an external entity such as a service provider.

- Gauging their organizational cybersecurity posture against the prioritized cybersecurity activities

5. Smart Grid Business/Mission Objectives

Development of the Smart Grid Profile included identification of common business objectives for the grid. These business objectives, which also accounted for regulatory and cybersecurity requirements, provide a useful context for identifying and managing applicable cybersecurity risks and mitigations. Four common business objectives for power systems stakeholders were identified: Maintain Safety; Maintain Power System Reliability; Maintain Power System Resilience; and Support Grid Modernization.

These business objectives are not listed in prioritized order and appear robust to changes in grid architecture or technology.

Maintain Safety

Safety is an overarching concern of power system management and seeks to minimize the impact to human life, equipment, and the environment from cybersecurity risks. This requirement aims to manage cybersecurity risks to safety.

Maintain Power System Reliability

Reliability is the ability to deliver stable and predictable power in expected conditions or, in case of power system failure, the ability to restore to a normal operational mode. For this Profile, reliability includes both sustained interruptions and momentary interruptions and can be measured in outage duration, frequency of outages, system availability, and response time. Reliability is intended to ensure predictable system performance (the system operates as intended) in sets of predetermined conditions which is defined as the system's expected operating environment. This requirement aims to manage cybersecurity risks to power system reliability.

Maintain Power System Resilience

Resilience is the ability to prepare for and adapt to changing conditions and withstand and gracefully recover from deliberate attacks, accidents, or naturally occurring threats or incidents. Resiliency engineering focuses on situations where the environmental conditions have deliberately been manipulated by malefactors [8]. This requirement aims to manage cybersecurity risks to power system resilience.

In regard to power systems, resilience is the ability of the system to withstand instability, unexpected conditions or faults, and gracefully return to predictable, but possibly degraded, performance.

Support Grid Modernization

The integration of smart devices into the grid should provide required power to customers, deliver reliable and accurate measurement data to control systems, and cause minimum disruptions when devices fail. These smart devices are cyber-physical systems that are increasingly being interconnected to the power distribution system to provide energy and ancillary services. However, distribution power systems were not originally designed to handle dispersed sources of generation, and these advanced systems may not be under direct management of or subject to the security policies and procedures of the power system owner/operator [9]. Additionally, grid modernization efforts will take decades. During this time, legacy and new devices will need to co-exist and interact safely and securely. This requirement supports integration of smart technologies with the traditional grid by managing cybersecurity risks to power system, including integrity and timeliness of data and control commands.

To align cybersecurity activities with overall organizational mission success, Subcategories were identified and prioritized to support these business objectives. This is intended to help power system owners/operators prioritize actions and resources.

The tables below highlight Subcategory outcomes that directly support achieving the identified business objectives. The selection of Subcategories for each business objective was based on a broad range of considerations for Smart Grid architectures. The most critical Subcategories may differ for individual power system owners/operators.

While not all Subcategories were selected for each business objective, users of this document are encouraged to consider all Subcategories in light of their own risk tolerance, risk appetite, asset management approach, and specific business objectives. For the purposes of this document, when a Subcategory is not selected for a specific business objective, it indicates that the activity may not directly assist power system owners/operators in meeting the specific business objective(s).

In developing this profile, the following considerations were identified:

- Most of the Identify Function addresses organizational activities. As a result, most of the Categories and Subcategories within the Identify Function are executed at the organizational level, rather than at a system level or specific security architecture level. These Subcategory outcomes provide overall direction for security activities and apply broadly to all business goals. For this reason, nearly every Identify Subcategory was selected as directly supporting the achievement of the business objectives. Where a Subcategory was not selected, a rationale was provided explaining the decision.

- Whether an organization's infrastructure is traditional or modernized, the recommendations in the Cybersecurity Framework and in this Profile follow cybersecurity best practices. Power system owners/operators should review each of the prioritized Subcategories in light of their own risk management processes and determine whether and how those Subcategories apply to their environment. Power system owners/operators should examine each Subcategory in terms of the impact not only to their organization, but also to interconnected organizations and surrounding communities. The recommendations in this Profile should be considered within the context of the size and interconnectedness of the power system owner/operator.

- In Smart Grid environments, power system owners/operators rely on and interact with a larger community of diverse third parties than in the traditional grid environments. These third parties include but are not limited to vendors, suppliers, contractors, distributed generation owners/operators, and consumers. Many of the Subcategories that power system owners/operators traditionally implemented within their own infrastructures will need to be extended to the third party-owned devices and infrastructures that interconnect with the power system infrastructure. Furthermore, supply chain risk management considerations are important in these relationships especially when smart grid devices and systems interoperate with third parties. In addition to using a variety of Subcategories in this document to help manage risks associated with third parties, power system owners/operators may consult Cybersecurity Procurement Language for Energy Delivery Systems [10] and Utilities Technology Council (UTC) white paper [11] for more specific guidance.

Identify - The Identify Function is critical in the development of the foundation for cybersecurity management, and in the understanding of cyber risk to systems, assets, data, and capabilities. This Function guides the owner/operator in the development of the foundation for cybersecurity management, and in the understanding of cyber risk to systems, assets, data, and capabilities. The activities in Asset Management, Business Environment, Risk Assessment, Risk Management Strategy, and Supply Chain Risk Management are the primary security areas that address protections for the four business objectives. The Subcategories below are derived from the Cybersecurity Framework Core, which includes descriptions and informative references for each Subcategory.

Table 3 - IDENTIFY Subcategories Prioritization and Considerations

	ID	Maintain Safety	Maintain Reliability	Maintain Resilience	Support Grid Modernization	Considerations for Power System Owners/Operators
Category			Subcategories			
Asset Management		ID.AM-1	ID.AM-1	ID.AM-1	ID.AM-1	Knowing hardware assets is critical for maintaining safety, reliability, and resilience, as well as facilitating the transition to the modern grid. Legacy and modernized assets[10] need to be known and understood. As modernized grids become more distributed, power system owners/operators need to be accountable for all distributed assets that they own.
		ID.AM-2	ID.AM-2	ID.AM-2	ID.AM-2	Knowing software assets is critical for maintaining reliability, and resilience, as well as facilitating the transition to the modern grid. Legacy and modernized assets need to be known and understood. This especially applies to modernized assets because the sophisticated logic that they execute is driven by software.
		ID.AM-3	ID.AM-3	ID.AM-3	ID.AM-3	Understanding communication and data flows is important to ensure reliability and resilience. Communications networks are critical for modernized grids, and understanding the different types of data flows (control, monitoring, and management) will provide critical information for managing those flows within modernized infrastructures and between modernized and traditional infrastructure.

---

[10] Modernized assets/devices refers to power system devices that utilize two-way communication technologies and advanced sensing capabilities to help improve grid operations.

	Maintain Safety	Maintain Reliability	Maintain Resilience	Support Grid Modernization	Considerations for Power System Owners/Operators
Category		Subcategories			
		ID.AM-4	ID.AM-4	ID.AM-4	The presence of external information systems may have many impacts on the power grid. Grid reliability and resilience may be impacted if power system owners/operators are not aware of all power systems, customer-owned devices, and any other third-party systems connected to the distribution system. With respect to supporting grid modernization, traditional and modernized parts of the grid will exist side by side within a single power system owner/operator and across power system ownership lines. Awareness of external information systems that manage both traditional and modernized components is important to assure security of both Information Technology (IT) and Operational Technology (OT) infrastructures.
	ID.AM-5	ID.AM-5	ID.AM-5	ID.AM-5	Power systems contain many types of resources, including devices, data, personnel, and software. Resources directly involved in the distribution of power should be prioritized ahead of business systems.
	ID.AM-6	ID.AM-6	ID.AM-6	ID.AM-6	Identifying all power system stakeholders and their roles and responsibilities with respect to maintaining and restoring power is critical to all four business requirements.
Business Environment		ID.BE-1	ID.BE-1	ID.BE-1	"Supply chain" in this Subcategory includes IT and OT products and services business partners, and other relevant third parties that support power delivery. As such it impacts the reliable flow of power and resiliency efforts including the flow of power from modernized parts of the grid.

Category	Maintain Safety	Maintain Reliability	Maintain Resilience	Support Grid Modernization	Considerations for Power System Owners/Operators
Subcategories					
	ID.BE-2	ID.BE-2	ID.BE-2	ID.BE-2	Power system owners/operators should understand their organization's placement in the grid infrastructure in order to manage potential cascading effects on the grid. The magnitude of potential cascading effects should be understood. Because the modernized grid incorporates distributed generation, the points of integration of distributed resources with the larger grid should be well understood. These pointes of integration may include generation, transmission, distribution, customers, and third-party owners/operators of distributed resources.
	ID.BE-3	ID.BE-3	ID.BE-3	ID.BE-3	Power system owners/operators have a variety of state and local regulatory requirements that influence their mission and objectives. See ID.GV-3.
	ID.BE-4	ID.BE-4	ID.BE-4	ID.BE-4	Understanding power system dependencies helps maintain reliability and resilience. It also facilitates grid modernization through providing necessary information to plan and implement grid modernization initiatives. Having a thorough understanding of dependencies within the power system can also improve safety. Identify all sources and loads that require power. Understand information about the loads, sources, and power delivery network at any given time. Use this information to control the flow of power from source to loads.
	ID.BE-5	ID.BE-5	ID.BE-5	ID.BE-5	Power system owners/operators should understand and implement the specific requirements to ensure resilient operation of the power system.

Category	Subcategories				Considerations for Power System Owners/Operators
	Maintain Safety	Maintain Reliability	Maintain Resilience	Support Grid Modernization	
Governance	ID.GV-1	ID.GV-1	ID.GV-1	ID.GV-1	Information security policy drives a set of coherent security requirements throughout the organization. In this context, security policy should support safety, reliability, resilience, privacy, and other related concerns. Also within this context, grid components are cyber-physical systems (CPS) themselves, composed into a more complex, networked cyber-physical system of systems. NIST CPS Public Working Group (PWG) Framework provides a set of relevant concerns. Organizational informational security policy should address OT and IT environments and how they integrate, the complexity of external partnerships, as well as cover both traditional and modernized environments.
	ID.GV-2	ID.GV-2	ID.GV-2	ID.GV-2	Information security roles and responsibilities and their coordination with external partners directly affect all requirements. In the context of the modernized grid, external parties include the owners of distributed resources.
	ID.GV-3	ID.GV-3	ID.GV-3	ID.GV-3	Legal and regulatory requirements regarding cybersecurity are especially applicable in the highly regulated critical infrastructure environment of electric power generation, transmission, and distribution. The modernized grid has additional regulatory requirements that should be considered here.
	ID.GV-4	ID.GV-4	ID.GV-4	ID.GV-4	Because the grid is a large cyber-physical system, governance and risk management processes should address all risks, not just cybersecurity.
Risk Assessment	ID.RA-1	ID.RA-1	ID.RA-1	ID.RA-1	Identifying and documenting asset vulnerabilities can be performed as part of a risk assessment. Vulnerabilities from traditional and modernized environments should be included, especially cyber-physical devices in the modern grid.

Category	Maintain Safety	Maintain Reliability	Maintain Resilience	Support Grid Modernization	Considerations for Power System Owners/Operators
Subcategories					
	ID.RA-2	ID.RA-2	ID.RA-2		Modernized devices need to be included in information sharing. However, these newer devices that are a part of grid modernization are not yet well-addressed within the information sharing forums of the power system owner/operator community.
	ID.RA-3	ID.RA-3	ID.RA-3	ID.RA-3	Potential threats are greatly increased in the more complex environment of the modernized grid, thereby requiring more extensive analysis. The environment is more complex because 1) the high number of devices exponentially increases the attack surface; 2) these devices may have different and distributed ownership; 3) the devices are likely heterogeneous; 4) the overall high interconnectivity of the modernized grid.
	ID.RA-4	ID.RA-4	ID.RA-4	ID.RA-4	The modernized grid will have additional and more complex business impacts due to its distributed and multi-owner nature and complex regulatory landscape.
	ID.RA-5	ID.RA-5	ID.RA-5	ID.RA-5	Power systems owners/operators should consider threats, vulnerabilities, and impacts to the converged IT/OT environment, including traditional and modernized components.
	ID.RA-6	ID.RA-6	ID.RA-6	ID.RA-6	The complexity of the stakeholder landscape in the modernized grid can make the risk responses of power system owners/operators more complicated. Power system owners/operators will need to consider how proposed risk responses will impact interconnected stakeholders.
Risk Management Strategy	ID.RM-1	ID.RM-1	ID.RM-1	ID.RM-1	The complexity of the stakeholder landscape in the modernized grid can make risk management processes more complicated.
	ID.RM-2	ID.RM-2	ID.RM-2	ID.RM-2	Power system owners/operators should consider the development of a comprehensive strategy to manage risk, including integrating the modernized components of the grid into the determination and description of risk tolerance.

Category	Maintain Safety	Maintain Reliability	Maintain Resilience	Support Grid Modernization	Considerations for Power System Owners/Operators
	Subcategories				
	ID.RM-3	ID.RM-3	ID.RM-3	ID.RM-3	When determining organizational risk tolerance, power system owners/operators should consider the potential cascading effects on the immediate geographic area, larger region, and the sector overall.
Supply Chain Risk Management		ID.SC-1	ID.SC-1	ID.SC-1	Power system owners/operators rely on integrators, Industrial Control System (ICS) vendors, and commercial off-the-shelf (COTS) providers to design and implement networks, systems, and applications that run the grid. As power systems owners/operators modernize their grids, their supply chains increasingly include third party service providers and distributed generation owners/operators. Power system owners/operators therefore need to have robust processes for managing cybersecurity risks stemming from these supply chains that include all relevant members of this diverse ecosystem.
		ID.SC-2	ID.SC-2	ID.SC-2	Organizational supply chain risk management processes should be continuously improved regardless of the environment being traditional or modernized.
	ID.SC-3	ID.SC-3	ID.SC-3	ID.SC-3	When power systems transcend organizational boundaries, it may be beneficial for power system owners/operators to mutually agree on a set of appropriate security requirements in order to manage security risks. In addition to security requirements in supplier agreements, power system owners/operators are encouraged to establish a set of security requirements with their third-party partners. These agreements may be mutual, as in power system owners/operators would also be agreeing to a set of security requirements they would commit to abide by. This is a key risk management consideration for power system owners/operators.

	Maintain Safety	Maintain Reliability	Maintain Resilience	Support Grid Modernization	Considerations for Power System Owners/Operators
Category		Subcategories			
	ID.SC-4	ID.SC-4	ID.SC-4	ID.SC-4	Assessments are required to understand whether suppliers and third parties are continuously following agreed-upon cybersecurity requirements. Power system owners/operators should consider that lack of these assurances can have an impact on all critical business/mission goals.
	ID.SC-5	ID.SC-5	ID.SC-5	ID.SC-5	Power system owners/operators should ensure that the modernized (including distributed) power environment is accounted for in response and recovery plans. Testing of these plans helps manage grid modernization efforts. Additionally, suppliers and 3rd-party providers should be included in testing of these plans. Suppliers and 3rd-party providers are critical to orderly restoration after incidents. If they are not properly integrated in testing efforts, it may have an impact on all critical business/mission goals.

Protect – The Protect Function is critical to limit the impact of a potential cybersecurity event. Identity Management and Access Control, Awareness and Training, Information Protection Processes, Maintenance, and Protective Technology are the priority security focus areas. Identity Management and Access Control identifies and regulates personnel ingress and egress. Awareness and Training and the Protection Processes prepare the workforce to achieve cyber security. Protective technology implements security decisions. The Subcategories below are derived from the Cybersecurity Framework Core, which includes descriptions and informative references for each Subcategory.

Table 4 - PROTECT Subcategories Prioritization and Considerations

		Maintain Safety	Maintain Reliability	Maintain Resilience	Support Grid Modernization	Considerations for Power Systems Owners/Operators
Category		Subcategories				
		PR.AC-1	PR.AC-1	PR.AC-1	PR.AC-1	Identity management is essential for all users, devices, and processes in both traditional and modernized environments.
		PR.AC-2	PR.AC-2	PR.AC-2	PR.AC-2	Power system owners/operators should control physical access to the power system components as needed, including modernized and distributed grid components. Power system owners/operators should consider the limitations of maintaining physical access to devices on other premises, especially those devices that are owned by a 3rd party.
PR	Access Control	PR.AC-3	PR.AC-3	PR.AC-3	PR.AC-3	Many grid components are maintained remotely and such remote access should be secured. For modernized environments, consider the limitations of managing remote access to devices that are owned by a 3rd party, such as distributed resources.
		PR.AC-4	PR.AC-4	PR.AC-4	PR.AC-4	Least privilege is important for limiting permissions and authorizations to manage connected devices. This reduces risks of unapproved operations which may create negative impacts to safety, reliability, and resilience. For example, excessive privileges may create an opportunity for compromise during power restoration. Grid modernization efforts should ensure that least privilege principles are designed into and implemented in the modernized grid.

22

Category	Subcategories				Considerations for Power Systems Owners/Operators
	Maintain Safety	Maintain Reliability	Maintain Resilience	Support Grid Modernization	
	PR.AC-5	PR.AC-5	PR.AC-5	PR.AC-5	Network segmentation is an important tool for containing potential incidents (safety, reliability), and limiting damage from incidents (resilience). Grid modernization efforts should consider segmenting networks from the design stage into operations (e.g., DER devices could be segmented to limit exposure to the rest of the power system infrastructure).
	PR.AC-6	PR.AC-6	PR.AC-6	PR.AC-6	In the power system, the safe delivery of reliable power is paramount. For this reason, there may be situations (e.g., emergency maintenance or need to restore power) in which the binding and proofing of credentials may interfere with safety, reliability, and resilience. Power system owners/operators will need to consider any risks introduced if identities are not proofed and bound to credentials and if those credentials are not required for certain user actions.
	PR.AC-7	PR.AC-7	PR.AC-7	PR.AC-7	Devices should be authenticated before connecting to the grid network to ensure that only authorized devices are allowed to connect. Proper authentication of users, devices, and assets helps ensure safety and reliability. Special care will need to be taken to ensure that modernized devices are also authenticated to the grid network.
Awareness and Training	PR.AT-1	PR.AT-1	PR.AT-1	PR.AT-1	User training needs to include a mention that modernization of a grid has impact to cybersecurity. For example, the dependence on bi-directional, real-time data flows increases the importance of data integrity. Security awareness training should be provided to all users, including manufacturing system users and managers. Training could include, for example, a basic understanding of the protections and user actions needed to maintain security of the system, procedures for responding to suspected cybersecurity incidents, and awareness of operational security. Also, it is recommended to incorporate threat recognition and reporting into security awareness training.

Category	Subcategories				Considerations for Power Systems Owners/Operators
	Maintain Safety	Maintain Reliability	Maintain Resilience	Support Grid Modernization	
	PR.AT-2	PR.AT-2	PR.AT-2	PR.AT-2	Privileged user training needs to include a mention that legacy to non-legacy migration has impact to cybersecurity. For example, the dependence on bi-directional, real-time data flows increases the importance of data integrity.
	PR.AT-3	PR.AT-3	PR.AT-3	PR.AT-3	The stakeholder landscape is complicated in the modernized grid and power system owners/operators will need to include roles and responsibilities of all relevant stakeholders, including third parties.
	PR.AT-4	PR.AT-4	PR.AT-4	PR.AT-4	Executives need to understand the implications of business decisions (e.g., grid modernization) on cybersecurity—which can impact the larger business/mission goals
	PR.AT-5	PR.AT-5	PR.AT-5	PR.AT-5	Training and responsibilities for physical and information security personnel need to be tailored to the unique threats and risks of the grid modernization environment as well as the distributed and multi-owner nature of the environment.
Data Security	PR.DS-1	PR.DS-1			In the case of power grid systems, protecting data-at-rest should apply to protecting the integrity of device settings. If tampered with, device settings may cause a safety or reliability issue.

Category	Maintain Safety	Maintain Reliability	Maintain Resilience	Support Grid Modernization	Considerations for Power Systems Owners/Operators
Subcategories					
	PR.DS-2	PR.DS-2	PR.DS-2	PR.DS-2	In the case of power grid systems, protecting data in-transit is an important tool to help protect the integrity of control information and device settings. Loss of integrity of control information may cause a safety or reliability issue. Power system owners/operators should consider the potential for resource-intensive cryptographic mechanisms to interfere with the functional performance of control systems and use additional methods to protect data in transit when less resource intensive cryptographic mechanisms are used.
	PR.DS-3	PR.DS-3	PR.DS-3	PR.DS-3	Power system owners/operators need to be aware of all distributed, modernized assets they own and manage them throughout the life cycle. IT components embedded in OT devices within the grid modernization infrastructure (e.g., power control and delivery) may present challenges of ownership/contractual agreements with the manufacturers. During disposal of assets, special care should be taken to not expose device configuration data. The integrity of device configuration data should be protected to not impact future safety and reliability.
	PR.DS-4	PR.DS-4	PR.DS-4	PR.DS-4	Understanding capacity requirements is critical for power system reliability and resilience.
	PR.DS-5	PR.DS-5	PR.DS-5	PR.DS-5	Data can be used to understand system behavior and devise methods to attack the system. Therefore, protection from data leaks is important for safety and reliability.
	PR.DS-6	PR.DS-6	PR.DS-6	PR.DS-6	The integrity of information and of software/firmware running on system components is critical to all business/mission requirements.

Category	Maintain Safety	Maintain Reliability	Maintain Resilience	Support Grid Modernization	Considerations for Power Systems Owners/Operators
	Subcategories				
	PR.DS-7	PR.DS-7	PR.DS-7		The separation of development and testing environments is critical to ensure testing does not accidentally impact operational systems. Therefore, insufficient separation could directly impact safety, reliability, and resilience. This applies to both traditional and modernized environments equally; therefore, grid modernization is not specifically highlighted. This should be already done for the traditional environment and this good process should also apply to modernized environments. However, it should be noted that applying this to distributed environments may be challenging due to their scope.
	PR.DS-8	PR.DS-8	PR.DS-8	PR.DS-8	The integrity of power system hardware is critical to safety, reliability, resilience, and grid modernization.
Information Protection Processes and Procedures	PR.IP-1	PR.IP-1	PR.IP-1	PR.IP-1	Baseline configurations are needed for all devices that are owned by a power system owner/operator. However, power system owner/operators should consider that they may have little or no control over the configuration of devices owned by other stakeholders connecting to the grid. Creating and maintaining baseline configurations supports the safety, reliability, and resilience (known state to restore to) of the power grid. Grid modernization efforts are also supported by having a standard configuration for all modernized devices.
	PR.IP-2	PR.IP-2			Implementing a systems development life cycle ensures quality and predictable performance of systems and networks. It is critical for safety and reliability. While also important for resilience and grid modernization, it is in no way special for those two goals which are thus not selected.
	PR.IP-3	PR.IP-3	PR.IP-3	PR.IP-3	Configuration change control processes support safety, reliability, resilience (known state to restore to), and transition to modernized grid. Power system owners/operators should consider how organizational configuration change control processes will include devices owned by third parties

Category	Maintain Safety	Maintain Reliability	Maintain Resilience	Support Grid Modernization	Considerations for Power Systems Owners/Operators
		Subcategories			
	PR.IP-4	PR.IP-4	PR.IP-4	PR.IP-4	Backups are essential for retaining device configuration information so that devices can be restored and recovered to proper operational states. Modernized grids are especially susceptible because modern devices have more programmable logic in them. Special consideration should be taken to address backups of devices owned by third parties.
	PR.IP-5	PR.IP-5	PR.IP-5	PR.IP-5	Physical security policies are important for safety and reliability of the power grid. Physical access to sensors can lead to sensors being used as attack vectors. Physical security policies also support the integration of distributed, modernized devices into the grid.
	PR.IP-6	PR.IP-6	PR.IP-6	PR.IP-6	The destruction of data is not directly applicable to these business/mission requirements.
	PR.IP-7	PR.IP-7	PR.IP-7	PR.IP-7	Protection processes should be continuously improved regardless of whether the power system environment is traditional or modernized.
	PR.IP-8	PR.IP-8	PR.IP-8	PR.IP-8	Sharing the effectiveness of protection technologies is not directly applicable to these business/mission requirements.
	PR.IP-9	PR.IP-9	PR.IP-9	PR.IP-9	Power system owners/operators need to be sure to include the modernized environment/devices in the response and recovery plans and their testing to help manage grid modernization efforts. They should also ensure that the plans address the collaboration between IT and OT personnel and the distributed nature of modernized environments.
	PR.IP-10	PR.IP-10	PR.IP-10	PR.IP-10	Power system owners/operators need to be sure to include the modernized environment/devices in cybersecurity response and recovery plans and their testing to help manage grid modernization efforts. The plans need to address the collaboration between IT and OT personnel as well as the distributed nature of modernized environments.

Category	Maintain Safety	Maintain Reliability	Maintain Resilience	Support Grid Modernization	Considerations for Power Systems Owners/Operators
	Subcategories				
	PR.IP-11	PR.IP-11	PR.IP-11		Processes and procedures for including cybersecurity in human resources practices are the same for both traditional and modernized environments. Therefore, no special accommodations are required for the modernized grid.
	PR.IP-12	PR.IP-12	PR.IP-12	PR.IP-12	Modernized distributed energy resources can have vulnerabilities that may allow new and unaccounted threat vectors to the power grid. Power system owners/operators should consider how externally-owned devices and third-party owners/operators will be included in a vulnerability management plan.
Maintenance	PR.MA-1	PR.MA-1	PR.MA-1	PR.MA-1	Special care needs to be taken when devices are owned by third parties as may be the case in modernized environments.
Maintenance	PR.MA-2	PR.MA-2	PR.MA-2	PR.MA-2	Power system owners/operators need to be aware of any remote access capabilities that the device vendor may have to equipment. This is extremely important in energy environments due to distributed nature, geographical dispersion, and the mission need for remote maintenance of both legacy and modernized devices.
Protective Technology	PR.PT-1	PR.PT-1	PR.PT-1	PR.PT-1	Audit logs capture information that will be helpful during an attack to find anomalies and potentially limit the impact or stop the incident from inflicting worse damage (helps safety). Capturing and monitoring audit logs is also important for managing cybersecurity risks to grid modernization. These audit logs may provide visibility into the activities and traffic related to these distributed devices.
Protective Technology	PR.PT-2	PR.PT-2	PR.PT-2		Protecting and restricting the use of removable media on modernized devices has the same considerations as on legacy devices.
Protective Technology	PR.PT-3	PR.PT-3	PR.PT-3	PR.PT-3	Power system owners/operators should consider how the principle of least functionality will be applied to third-party assets connected to their grid.

Category		Maintain Safety	Maintain Reliability	Maintain Resilience	Support Grid Modernization	Considerations for Power Systems Owners/Operators
	Subcategories					
		PR.PT-4	PR.PT-4	PR.PT-4	PR.PT-4	Distributed multi-ownership of some modern grid (e.g., DER) environments may make it challenging to protect communications and control networks.
		PR.PT-5	PR.PT-5	PR.PT-5	PR.PT-5	Power system owners/operators should consider all possible ways to achieve resiliency requirements.

Detect – The Detect Function enables timely discovery of cybersecurity events. Real time awareness and continuous monitoring of the systems is critical to detect cybersecurity events. The Subcategories below are derived from the Cybersecurity Framework Core, which includes descriptions and informative references for each Subcategory.

Table 5 - DETECT Subcategories Prioritization and Considerations

Category	Maintain Safety	Maintain Reliability	Maintain Resilience	Support Grid Modernization	Considerations for Power Systems Owners/Operators
	Subcategories				
DE Anomalies and Events	DE.AE-1	DE.AE-1	DE.AE-1	DE.AE-1	A baseline of network operations and expected data flows is extremely important in the OT space because information flows are predictable, and control systems generally have few users. Understanding the control information flows will help monitor and detect unusual network behavior and allow for timely response. This applies to both traditional and modernized grid environments.
	DE.AE-2	DE.AE-2	DE.AE-2	DE.AE-2	Analyzing detected cybersecurity events is critical for safety, reliability, and resilience. There are no special considerations for modernized parts of the infrastructure.
	DE.AE-3	DE.AE-3	DE.AE-3	DE.AE-3	When collecting and aggregating data from third-party devices, the devices and the data should be authenticated and validated. Without this authentication and validation, power system owners/operators should carefully consider whether those devices and their data can be trusted.
	DE.AE-4	DE.AE-4	DE.AE-4	DE.AE-4	Determining the impact of detected cybersecurity events is critical for safety, reliability, and resilience. There are no special considerations for modernized parts of the infrastructure.
	DE.AE-5	DE.AE-5	DE.AE-5	DE.AE-5	Establishing incident alert thresholds is critical for safety, reliability, and resilience. This practice applies to both traditional and modernized parts of the grid.

Category	Maintain Safety	Maintain Reliability	Maintain Resilience	Support Grid Modernization	Considerations for Power Systems Owners/Operators
		Subcategories			
Security Continuous Monitoring	DE.CM-1	DE.CM-1	DE.CM-1	DE.CM-1	Neglecting to monitor the grid for cybersecurity events may result in missing an event with implications and impact. For grid modernization, monitoring has to be built in for the future. While the selection of safety may be surprising, not monitoring substantially increases the risk of not knowing that there may be safety impacts and being unable to reduce or eliminate them.
	DE.CM-2	DE.CM-2	DE.CM-2	DE.CM-2	Monitoring the physical environment for cybersecurity events is critical for safety, reliability, and resilience. There are no special considerations for modernized parts of the infrastructure.
	DE.CM-3	DE.CM-3	DE.CM-3	DE.CM-3	Monitoring personnel activity for cybersecurity events is critical for safety, reliability, and resilience. There are no special considerations for modernized parts of the infrastructure.
	DE.CM-4	DE.CM-4	DE.CM-4	DE.CM-4	Power system owners/operators should consider applying malicious code detection methodologies to both traditional and modernized infrastructure. These devices contain complex software which makes them vulnerable to cyber attacks.
	DE.CM-5	DE.CM-5	DE.CM-5	DE.CM-5	Detecting unauthorized mobile code is critical for safety, reliability, and resilience. There are no special considerations for modernized parts of the infrastructure.
	DE.CM-6	DE.CM-6	DE.CM-6	DE.CM-6	Power system owners/operators rely on vendors and external service providers for many capabilities, including industrial control systems and communications networks required to operate the grid. Whether service providers are accessing IT or especially OT environments, those activities should be monitored to ensure mitigating actions can be taken in case of attack stemming from external connections.

Category	Maintain Safety	Maintain Reliability	Maintain Resilience	Support Grid Modernization	Considerations for Power Systems Owners/Operators
		Subcategories			
	DE.CM-7	DE.CM-7	DE.CM-7	DE.CM-7	Unauthorized personnel, connections, devices, or software introduce risks into IT and OT, and may impact grid operations. Any connections to IT and OT systems and networks should be authenticated to ensure that only approved and trusted parties gain access to those systems and networks.
	DE.CM-8	DE.CM-8	DE.CM-8	DE.CM-8	Performing vulnerability scans is required to identify vulnerabilities in critical infrastructure. For modernized environments, power system owners/operators may need to consider an agreement to scan 3rd party-owned devices that are connected to their grid.
Detection Processes	DE.DP-1	DE.DP-1	DE.DP-1	DE.DP-1	Knowing roles and responsibilities with respect to detection is critical to all four business goals. This includes restoration across power system ownership lines and within a single power system owner/operator with traditional and modernized components and networks. Distributed resources owners/operators may also have a role and responsibilities in detection activities.
	DE.DP-2	DE.DP-2	DE.DP-2	DE.DP-2	Power system owners/operators need to ensure that detection activities comply with jurisdiction-specific safety requirements.
	DE.DP-3	DE.DP-3	DE.DP-3	DE.DP-3	Power system owners/operators should consider any potential negative impact to the power system due to testing of detection processes. The owners/operators of distributed modernized devices may also need to participate in this testing.
	DE.DP-4	DE.DP-4	DE.DP-4	DE.DP-4	Event detection information communication includes communicating detection events across traditional and modernized environments as well as between power system owners/operators in the modernized grid.
	DE.DP-5	DE.DP-5	DE.DP-5	DE.DP-5	Detection processes should be continuously improved.

Respond – The Respond Function supports the ability to contain the impact of a potential cybersecurity event. Rapid and effective response and communication to cyber incidents is critical in protecting personnel and environmental safety. Situational awareness to the event unfolding is needed to properly address it. The Subcategories below are derived from the Cybersecurity Framework Core, which includes descriptions and informative references for each Subcategory.

Table 6 - RESPOND Subcategories Prioritization and Considerations

		Maintain Safety	Maintain Reliability	Maintain Resilience	Support Grid Modernization	Considerations for Power Systems Owners/Operators
	Category		Subcategories			
	Response Planning	RS.RP-1	RS.RP-1	RS.RP-1	RS.RP-1	Response plan execution applies in both traditional and modernized environments.
		RS.CO-1	RS.CO-1	RS.CO-1	RS.CO-1	Knowing roles and responsibilities with respect to response and grid restoration is critical to all four business goals. This includes restoration across power system ownership lines and within a single power system owner/operator with integration of traditional and modernized components and networks.
RS	Communications	RS.CO-2	RS.CO-2	RS.CO-2	RS.CO-2	Having an established criterion for reporting incidents helps support safety objectives to ensure that safety considerations are a part of incident response. Furthermore, resilience benefits from a thoughtful criterion.
		RS.CO-3	RS.CO-3	RS.CO-3	RS.CO-3	Assuming that the event response information is shared once an incident has occurred, this Subcategory outcome supports resilience, rather than reliability. Sharing of information is important to ensure safety of restoration crews and has to be executed across traditional and modernized systems and components.

Category	Subcategories				Considerations for Power Systems Owners/Operators
	Maintain Safety	Maintain Reliability	Maintain Resilience	Support Grid Modernization	
	RS.CO-4	RS.CO-4	RS.CO-4	RS.CO-4	Power system owners/operators should consider that the modernized grid is expected to have an expanded set of stakeholders that includes distributed resources owners/operators.
				RS.CO-5	Sharing information across power system boundaries is important, especially when some of the power systems are modernized and some are not. In this context, external stakeholders are assumed to include neighboring power system owners/operators.
Analysis	RS.AN-1	RS.AN-1	RS.AN-1		Investigating notifications from detection systems is important for safety, reliability, and resilience. There are no special considerations for modernized parts of the infrastructure.
	RS.AN-2	RS.AN-2	RS.AN-2	RS.AN-2	Power system owners/operators should take care to understand any similarities and differences in impacts between the traditional and modernized environments.
	RS.AN-3		RS.AN-3		Performing forensics of incidents is critical for safety and resilience.
	RS.AN-4		RS.AN-4		Categorizing incidents is critical for safety and resilience.
		RS.AN-5	RS.AN-5	RS.AN-5	Having processes for receiving and analyzing vulnerability information is important for reliability, resilience, and the modernized grid because devices in the modernized grid are smarter than the legacy devices and have their own vulnerabilities. Safety will benefit indirectly from these activities.
Mitigation	RS.MI-1		RS.MI-1		Containing incidents is critical for safety and resilience, since once an incident occurs, reliability has already been impacted. Containing incidents is important for both traditional and modernized infrastructures.

Category	Subcategories				Considerations for Power Systems Owners/Operators
	Maintain Safety	Maintain Reliability	Maintain Resilience	Support Grid Modernization	
Improvements	RS.MI-2	RS.MI-2	RS.MI-2	RS.MI-2	Mitigating incidents is critical for safety and resilience, since once an incident occurs, reliability has already been impacted. Mitigating incidents is important for both traditional and modernized infrastructures.
	RS.MI-3	RS.MI-3	RS.MI-3	RS.MI-3	Newer devices are likely to be more vulnerable because they are interconnected and more complex than legacy devices. Not patching will hinder the ability of power system owners/operators to be resilient and reliable. Processes should be in place to receive vulnerability information from vendors, as well as to share vulnerability information with device owners/operators across power systems that may have different ownership.
	RS.IM-1	RS.IM-1	RS.IM-1	RS.IM-1	Lessons learned will improve future safety, reliability, resilience, and grid modernization.
	RS.IM-2	RS.IM-2	RS.IM-2	RS.IM-2	Updating recovery strategies will improve future safety, reliability, resilience, and grid modernization.

Recover – The Recover Function supports timely recovery to normal operations to reduce the impact from a cybersecurity event. Defined Recovery objectives are needed when recovering from disruptions. The Subcategories below are derived from the Cybersecurity Framework Core, which includes descriptions and informative references for each Subcategory.

Table 7 - RECOVER Subcategories Prioritization and Considerations

Category	Subcategories				Considerations for Power Systems Owners/Operators
	Maintain Safety	Maintain Reliability	Maintain Resilience	Support Grid Modernization	
RE					
Recovery Planning	RC.RP-1	RC.RP-1	RC.RP-1	RC.RP-1	There are implications to safety of power system owner/operator workers (e.g., linemen) when the cyber security recovery plan is executed. The plan should include both traditional and modernized parts of the grid.
Improvements		RC.IM-1	RC.IM-1		Incorporating lessons learned into plans is absolutely critical for maintaining reliability and resilience. In this case the other two business goals are of secondary importance.
		RC.IM-2	RC.IM-2		Updating recovery strategies is critical for reliability and resilience and should cover any activities relevant to safety and grid modernization.
					While important, managing public relations is not critical for the four goals.
					While important, repairing reputation is not critical for the four goals.
Communications	RC.CO-3	RC.CO-3	RC.CO-3	RC.CO-3	Cyber security event recovery activities have to be coordinated to ensure safety of power system owner operator workers (e.g., linemen) working on power recovery. Recovery efforts also require coordination across power systems, some of which may be modernized and some not.

6. Future Work

This Smart Grid Profile effort focuses on identifying high level business/mission objectives of the smart grid and prioritizing Subcategory outcomes of the Cybersecurity Framework according to their ability to directly assist power system owners/operators in achieving those business/mission objectives. The Profile also provides power system owners/operators with considerations relevant to the challenges they may experience as they implement these cybersecurity activities in infrastructures with high concentrations of distributed energy resources (DERs).

This Profile looked at the smart grid from a high level to serve as a resource for those seeking to understand the basic application of cybersecurity concepts to the grid. Since this high-level view indicated that a large number of Subcategory outcomes was important to the grid, the considerations included for each Subcategory describe the grid relevance of the outcome. At a smart grid cybersecurity workshop held at NIST in November 2018, participants discussed the current risk Profile and ways to make it more useful to smart grid stakeholders. Those participant suggestions shape our future smart grid Profile work and are highlighted below.

The next version of the smart grid Profile will focus on cybersecurity considerations of a grid service/function rather than on an entire architecture. It was felt by participants that exploration of a service/function within the context of grid architecture would be more useful to stakeholders. To that end, we will compare and contrast the following:

- how a grid service or function is provided within a contemporary grid architecture and within the previously-explored High-DER architecture,

- by which stakeholders the service or function is delivered within each architecture, and

- cybersecurity considerations or concerns for stakeholders as they deliver the service or function within each architecture.

Similar to the current risk Profile effort, we will prioritize Cybersecurity Framework Subcategory outcomes for the grid service within each of the selected architectures. The prioritization of Cybersecurity Framework Subcategories is based on the Subcategory outcome's ability to directly assist in the delivery of the service within the examined architectures. Our goal will be to provide a more useful prioritization scale (e.g., low, medium, and high) for Subcategories rather than the binary (i.e., yes, no) scale used in the current effort.

Additionally, the next Profile will enable comparison of the Subcategory prioritization scales and cybersecurity considerations for stakeholders providing similar grid services within two different architectures. Finally, the goal is for the next Profile to contain updated mapping information between the Cybersecurity Framework v1.1 and the current North American Electric Reliability Corporation (NERC) Critical Infrastructure Protection (CIP) version.

References

[1]   United States, Executive Office of the President [Barack Obama]. Executive Order 13636: Improving Critical Infrastructure Cybersecurity. 12 Feb. 2013. *Federal Register*, vol. 78, 19 Feb. 2013, pp. 11737-44, https://www.federalregister.gov/d/2013-03915.

[2]   National Institute of Standards and Technology (2018) *Framework for Improving Critical Infrastructure Cybersecurity, version 1.1.* https:/doi.org/10.6028/NIST.CSWP.04162018

[3]   U.S. Department of Energy (2008) *Smart Grid: An Introduction.* Available at https://www.energy.gov/sites/prod/files/oeprod/DocumentsandMedia/DOE_SG_Book _Single_Pages%281%29.pdf

[4]   The Smart Grid Interoperability Panel – Smart Grid Cybersecurity Committee (2014) Guidelines for Smart Grid Cybersecurity [3 vols.]. (National Institute of Standards and Technology, Gaithersburg, MD), NIST Interagency Report (NIST IR) 7628, Rev. 1. https://doi.org/10.6028/NIST.IR.7628r1

[5]   Stouffer K, Pillitteri V, Lightman S, Abrams M, Hahn A (2015) Guide to Industrial Control Systems (ICS) Security. (National Institute of Standards and Technology, Gaithersburg, MD), NIST Special Publication (SP) 800-82, Rev. 2. https://doi.org/10.6028/NIST.SP.800-82r2

[6]   Taft JD (2016) Grid Architecture 2. (Pacific Northwest National Laboratory, Richland, WA), PNL-24044 2. Available at https://gridarchitecture.pnnl.gov/media/white-papers/GridArchitecture2final.pdf

[7]   Taft JD (2016) Advanced Networking Paradigms for High-DER Distribution Grids, version 3.0. (Pacific Northwest National Laboratory, Richland, WA), PNNL-25475. Available at https://gridarchitecture.pnnl.gov/media/advanced/Advanced%20Networking%20Para digms%20final.pdf

[8]   Cyber-Physical Systems Public Working Group (2017) Framework for Cyber-Physical Systems: Volume 2, Working Group Reports. (National Institute of Standards and Technology, Gaithersburg, MD), NIST Special Publication (SP) 1500-202, Version 1.0. https://doi.org/10.6028/NIST.SP.1500-202

[9]   International Electrotechnical Commission (2016) IEC TR 62351-12:2016 - *Power systems management and associated information exchange – Data and communication security – Part 12: Resilience and security recommendations for power systems with distributed energy resources (DER) cyber-physical systems* (IEC, Geneva, Switzerland). Available at https://webstore.iec.ch/publication/24474

[10]   Energy Sector Control Systems Working Group (2014) *Cybersecurity Procurement Language for Energy Delivery Systems*. Available at https://www.energy.gov/sites/prod/files/2014/04/f15/CybersecProcurementLanguage-EnergyDeliverySystems_040714_fin.pdf

[11]   Bartol N (2015) *Cyber Supply Chain Risk Management for Utilities – Roadmap for Implementation* (Utilities Telecom Council, Washington, DC). Available at https://utc.org/wp-content/uploads/2018/02/SupplyChain2015-2.pdf

[12]   Gopstein AM (2012) Energy Storage & the Grid—From Characteristics to Impact. *Institute of Electrical and Electronics Engineers (IEEE) Proceedings of the IEEE* 100(2):311-316. https://doi.org/10.1109/JPROC.2011.2174890

[13]   North American Electric Reliability Corporation, Critical Infrastructure Protection Committee, Control Systems Security Working Group (2014) Mapping of NIST Cybersecurity Framework to NERC CIP v3/v5 (North American Electric Reliability Corporation, Washington, DC). Available at https://www.nerc.com/comm/CIPC_Security_Guidelines_DL/CSSWG-Mapping_of_NIST_Cybersecurity_Framework_to_NERC_CIP.pdf

Appendix A: Acronyms

Selected acronyms and abbreviations used in this paper are defined below.

AMI   Advanced Metering Infrastructure

COTS   Commercial Off-the-Shelf

CSF

DoE

ICS   Industrial Control System

IEC   International Electrotechnical Commission

ISA   The International Society of Automation

IT   Information Technology

ITL   Information Technology Laboratory

LAN

NERC

OT

                  Utilities Telecom Council

Appendix B: NERC CIP v5 to Cybersecurity Framework v1.0 Mapping

The table below is the result of work by the NERC Critical Infrastructure Protection Committee (CIPC) Control Systems Security Working Group (CSSWG) to map Subcategory outcomes of the Cybersecurity Framework v1.0 to NERC CIP versions 3 and 5. This information supplements the Subcategory prioritization and considerations for power system owners/operators presented in Sec. 5 of this Profile. As owners/operators and electricity subsector cybersecurity practitioners consider the applicability of the information in Sec. 5 to their power systems, the mapping information below will help them ensure compliance with NERC CIP requirements. This mapping can also help them align with practices from the Department of Energy's Cybersecurity Capability Maturity Model (C2M2) Program.

It should be noted that the mapping information contained in this appendix was completed in November 2014. Since that time, both NERC CIP and the Cybersecurity Framework have been updated. Future Profile work aims to include updated mapping information to improve the usefulness to stakeholders. The mapping work completed by the CIPC CSSWG included one additional column which provided specific implementation guidance for the NERC CIP controls. For our Profile, we omitted that guidance column because our purpose was primarily to provide the Cybersecurity Framework v1.0 to NERC CIP mapping information.

Mapping of NIST Cybersecurity Framework v1.0 to NERC CIP version 5 & C2M2 Practices						
Function	Category	Subcategory	C2M2 Practices **			NERC CIP v5
			MIL 1	MIL 2	MIL 3	
IDENTIFY (ID)	**Asset Management (AM):** The data, personnel, devices, systems, and facilities that enable the organization to achieve business purposes are identified and managed consistent with their relative importance to business objectives and the organization's risk strategy.	**ID.AM-1:** Physical devices and systems within the organization are inventoried	ACM-1a	ACM-1c	ACM-1e ACM-1f	CIP-002-5.1 R1: Each Responsible Entity shall implement a process that considers each of the following assets for purposes of parts 1.1 through 1.3: i. Control Centers and backup Control Centers; ii. Transmission stations and substations; iii. Generation resources; iv. Systems and facilities critical to system restoration, including Blackstart Resources and Cranking Paths and initial switching requirements; v. Special Protection Systems that support the reliable operation of the Bulk Electric System (BES); and vi. For Distribution Providers, Protection Systems specified in Applicability section 4.2.1 above.

Mapping of NIST Cybersecurity Framework v1.0 to NERC CIP version 5 & C2M2 Practices

Function	Category	Subcategory	C2M2 Practices **			NERC CIP v5
			MIL 1	MIL 2	MIL 3	
IDENTIFY (ID)	**Asset Management (AM):** The data, personnel, devices, systems, and facilities that enable the organization to achieve business purposes are identified and managed consistent with their relative importance to business objectives and the organization's risk strategy.	**ID.AM-1:** Physical devices and systems within the organization are inventoried	ACM-1a	ACM-1c	ACM-1e ACM-1f	CIP-002-5.1 R2: The Responsible Entity shall: (2.1) Review the identifications in Requirement R1 and its parts (and update them if there are changes identified) at least once every 15 calendar months, even if it has no identified items in Requirement R1, and; (2.2) Have its CIP Senior Manager or delegate approve the identifications required by Requirement R1 at least once every 15 calendar months, even if it has no identified items in Requirement R1.
IDENTIFY (ID)	**Asset Management (AM):** The data, personnel, devices, systems, and facilities that enable the organization to achieve business purposes are identified and managed consistent with their relative importance to business objectives and the organization's risk strategy.	**ID.AM-1:** Physical devices and systems within the organization are inventoried	ACM-1a	ACM-1c	ACM-1e ACM-1f	CIP-003-5 R2: Each Responsible Entity for its assets identified in CIP-002-5, Requirement R1, Part R1.3, shall implement, in a manner that identifies, assesses, and corrects deficiencies, one or more documented cyber security policies that collectively address the following topics, and review and obtain CIP Senior Manager approval for those policies at least once every 15 calendar months: (An inventory, list, or discrete identification of low impact BES Cyber Systems or their BES Cyber Assets is not required). (2.1) Cyber security awareness; (2.2) Physical security controls; (2.3) Electronic access controls for external routable protocol connections and Dial-up Connectivity; and (2.4) Incident response to a Cyber Security Incident.

Mapping of NIST Cybersecurity Framework v1.0 to NERC CIP version 5 & C2M2 Practices

Function	Category	Subcategory	C2M2 Practices **			NERC CIP v5
			MIL 1	MIL 2	MIL 3	
IDENTIFY (ID)	**Asset Management (AM):** The data, personnel, devices, systems, and facilities that enable the organization to achieve business purposes are identified and managed consistent with their relative importance to business objectives and the organization's risk strategy.	**ID.AM-2:** Software platforms and applications within the organization are inventoried	ACM-1b	ACM-1c	ACM-1e ACM-1f	CIP-002-5.1 R1: Each Responsible Entity shall implement a process that considers each of the following assets for purposes of parts 1.1 through 1.3: i. Control Centers and backup Control Centers; ii. Transmission stations and substations; iii. Generation resources; iv. Systems and facilities critical to system restoration, including Blackstart Resources and Cranking Paths and initial switching requirements; v. Special Protection Systems that support the reliable operation of the Bulk Electric System; and vi. For Distribution Providers, Protection Systems specified in Applicability section 4.2.1 above.
IDENTIFY (ID)	**Asset Management (AM):** The data, personnel, devices, systems, and facilities that enable the organization to achieve business purposes are identified and managed consistent with their relative importance to business objectives and the organization's risk strategy.	**ID.AM-2:** Software platforms and applications within the organization are inventoried	ACM-1b	ACM-1c	ACM-1e ACM-1f	CIP-002-5.1 R2: The Responsible Entity shall: (2.1) Review the identifications in Requirement R1 and its parts (and update them if there are changes identified) at least once every 15 calendar months, even if it has no identified items in Requirement R1, and; (2.2) Have its CIP Senior Manager or delegate approve the identifications required by Requirement R1 at least once every 15 calendar months, even if it has no identified items in Requirement R1.

Mapping of NIST Cybersecurity Framework v1.0 to NERC CIP version 5 & C2M2 Practices

Function	Category	Subcategory	C2M2 Practices **			NERC CIP v5
			MIL 1	MIL 2	MIL 3	
IDENTIFY (ID)	**Asset Management (AM):** The data, personnel, devices, systems, and facilities that enable the organization to achieve business purposes are identified and managed consistent with their relative importance to business objectives and the organization's risk strategy.	**ID.AM-3:** Organizational communication and data flows are mapped		RM-2g	ACM-1e	CIP-002-5.1 R1: Each Responsible Entity shall implement a process that considers each of the following assets for purposes of parts 1.1 through 1.3: i. Control Centers and backup Control Centers; ii. Transmission stations and substations; iii. Generation resources; iv. Systems and facilities critical to system restoration, including Blackstart Resources and Cranking Paths and initial switching requirements; v. Special Protection Systems that support the reliable operation of the Bulk Electric System; and vi. For Distribution Providers, Protection Systems specified in Applicability section 4.2.1 above.
IDENTIFY (ID)	**Asset Management (AM):** The data, personnel, devices, systems, and facilities that enable the organization to achieve business purposes are identified and managed consistent with their relative importance to business objectives and the organization's risk strategy.	**ID.AM-3:** Organizational communication and data flows are mapped		RM-2g	ACM-1e	CIP-003-5 R1 - 1.2: Each Responsible Entity, for its high impact and medium impact BES Cyber Systems, shall review and obtain CIP Senior Manager approval at least once every 15 calendar months for one or more documented cyber security policies that collectively address the following topics: Electronic Security Perimeters (CIP-005) including Interactive Remote Access;
IDENTIFY (ID)	**Asset Management (AM):** The data, personnel, devices, systems, and facilities that enable the organization to achieve business purposes are identified and managed consistent with their relative importance to business objectives and the organization's risk strategy.	**ID.AM-3:** Organizational communication and data flows are mapped		RM-2g	ACM-1e	CIP-005-5 R2: Each Responsible Entity allowing Interactive Remote Access to BES Cyber Systems shall implement one or more documented processes that collectively include the applicable requirement parts, where technically feasible, in CIP-005-5 Table R2 – Interactive Remote Access Management.

44

Mapping of NIST Cybersecurity Framework v1.0 to NERC CIP version 5 & C2M2 Practices

Function	Category	Subcategory	C2M2 Practices **			NERC CIP v5
			MIL 1	MIL 2	MIL 3	
IDENTIFY (ID)	**Asset Management (AM):** The data, personnel, devices, systems, and facilities that enable the organization to achieve business purposes are identified and managed consistent with their relative importance to business objectives and the organization's risk strategy.	**ID.AM-3:** Organizational communication and data flows are mapped		RM-2g	ACM-1e	CIP-011-1 R1: Each Responsible Entity shall implement, in a Manner that identifies, assesses, and corrects deficiencies, one or more documented information protection program(s) that collectively includes each of the applicable requirement parts in CIP-011-1 Table R1 – Information Protection.
IDENTIFY (ID)	**Asset Management (AM):** The data, personnel, devices, systems, and facilities that enable the organization to achieve business purposes are identified and managed consistent with their relative importance to business objectives and the organization's risk strategy.	**ID.AM-4:** External information systems are catalogued	EDM-1a	EDM-1c EDM-1e	EDM-1g RM-1c	CIP-002-5.1 R1: Each Responsible Entity shall implement a process that considers each of the following assets for purposes of parts 1.1 through 1.3: i. Control Centers and backup Control Centers; ii. Transmission stations and substations; iii. Generation resources; iv. Systems and facilities critical to system restoration, including Blackstart Resources and Cranking Paths and initial switching requirements; v. Special Protection Systems that support the reliable operation of the Bulk Electric System; and vi. For Distribution Providers, Protection Systems specified in Applicability section 4.2.1 above.
IDENTIFY (ID)	**Asset Management (AM):** The data, personnel, devices, systems, and facilities that enable the organization to achieve business purposes are identified and managed consistent with their relative importance to business objectives and the organization's risk strategy.	**ID.AM-4:** External information systems are catalogued	EDM-1a	EDM-1c EDM-1e	EDM-1g RM-1c	CIP-002-5.1 R2: The Responsible Entity shall: (2.1) Review the identifications in Requirement R1 and its parts (and update them if there are changes identified) at least once every 15 calendar months, even if it has no identified items in Requirement R1, and; (2.2) Have its CIP Senior Manager or delegate approve the identifications required by Requirement R1 at least once every 15 calendar months, even if it has no identified items in Requirement R1.

			C2M2 Practices **			
Function	Category	Subcategory	MIL 1	MIL 2	MIL 3	NERC CIP v5

Mapping of NIST Cybersecurity Framework v1.0 to NERC CIP version 5 & C2M2 Practices						
IDENTIFY (ID)	**Asset Management (AM):** The data, personnel, devices, systems, and facilities that enable the organization to achieve business purposes are identified and managed consistent with their relative importance to business objectives and the organization's risk strategy.	**ID.AM-4:** External information systems are catalogued	EDM-1a	EDM-1c EDM-1e	EDM-1g RM-1c	CIP-003-5 R1 - 1.1 to 1.9: Each Responsible Entity, for its high impact and medium impact BES Cyber Systems, shall review and obtain CIP Senior Manager approval at least once every 15 calendar months for one or more documented cyber security policies that collectively address the following topics: 1.1 Personnel & training (CIP-004) 1.2 Electronic Security Perimeters (CIP005) including interactive Remote Access, 1.3 Physical Security of BES Cyber Systems (CIP006), 1.4 System security management (CIP007), 1.5 Incident reporting and response planning (CIP008), 1.6 Recovery plans for BES Cyber Systems (CIP009), 1.7 Configuration change management and vulnerability assessments (CIP010), 1.8 Information protection (CIP011) and 1.9 Declaring and responding to CIP Exceptional Circumstances.

Mapping of NIST Cybersecurity Framework v1.0 to NERC CIP version 5 & C2M2 Practices

Function	Category	Subcategory	C2M2 Practices **			NERC CIP v5
			MIL 1	MIL 2	MIL 3	
IDENTIFY (ID)	**Asset Management (AM):** The data, personnel, devices, systems, and facilities that enable the organization to achieve business purposes are identified and managed consistent with their relative importance to business objectives and the organization's risk strategy.	**ID.AM-4:** External information systems are catalogued	EDM-1a	EDM-1c EDM-1e	EDM-1g RM-1c	CIP-003 R2: Each Responsible Entity for its assets identified in CIP-002-5, Requirement R1, Part R1.3, shall implement, in a manner that identifies, assesses, and corrects deficiencies, one or more documented cyber security policies that collectively address the following topics, and review and obtain CIP Senior Manager approval for those policies at least once every 15 calendar months: [Violation Risk Factor: Lower] [Time Horizon: Operations Planning] 2.1 Cyber security awareness; 2.2 Physical security controls; 2.3 Electronic access controls for external routable protocol connections and Dial-up Connectivity; and 2.4 Incident response to a Cyber Security Incident. An inventory, list, or discrete identification of low impact BES Cyber Systems or their BES Cyber Assets is not required.
IDENTIFY (ID)	**Asset Management (AM):** The data, personnel, devices, systems, and facilities that enable the organization to achieve business purposes are identified and managed consistent with their relative importance to business objectives and the organization's risk strategy.	**ID.AM-4:** External information systems are catalogued	EDM-1a	EDM-1c EDM-1e	EDM-1g RM-1c	CIP-005-5 R1: Each Responsible Entity shall implement one or more documented processes that collectively include each of the applicable requirement parts in CIP-005-5 Table R1 – Electronic Security Perimeter.

		Mapping of NIST Cybersecurity Framework v1.0 to NERC CIP version 5 & C2M2 Practices				
			C2M2 Practices **			
Function	**Category**	**Subcategory**	**MIL 1**	**MIL 2**	**MIL 3**	**NERC CIP v5**
IDENTIFY (ID)	**Asset Management (AM):** The data, personnel, devices, systems, and facilities that enable the organization to achieve business purposes are identified and managed consistent with their relative importance to business objectives and the organization's risk strategy.	**ID.AM-5:** Resources (e.g., hardware, devices, data, and software) are prioritized based on their classification, criticality, and business value	ACM-1a ACM-1b	ACM-1c ACM-1d		CIP-002-5.1 R1: Each Responsible Entity shall implement a process that considers each of the following assets for purposes of parts 1.1 through 1.3: i. Control Centers and backup Control Centers; ii. Transmission stations and substations; iii. Generation resources; iv. Systems and facilities critical to system restoration, including Blackstart Resources and Cranking Paths and initial switching requirements; v. Special Protection Systems that support the reliable operation of the Bulk Electric System; and vi. For Distribution Providers, Protection Systems specified in Applicability section 4.2.1 above.
IDENTIFY (ID)	**Asset Management (AM):** The data, personnel, devices, systems, and facilities that enable the organization to achieve business purposes are identified and managed consistent with their relative importance to business objectives and the organization's risk strategy.	**ID.AM-5:** Resources (e.g., hardware, devices, data, and software) are prioritized based on their classification, criticality, and business value	ACM-1a ACM-1b	ACM-1c ACM-1d		CIP-003-5 R1 - 1.1 to 1.9: Each Responsible Entity, for its high impact and medium impact BES Cyber Systems, shall review and obtain CIP Senior Manager approval at least once every 15 calendar months for one or more documented cyber security policies that collectively address the following topics: 1.1 Personnel & training (CIP-004) 1.2 Electronic Security Perimeters (CIP005) including interactive Remote Access, 1.3 Physical Security of BES Cyber Systems (CIP006), 1.4 System security management (CIP007), 1.5 Incident reporting and response planning (CIP008), 1.6 Recovery plans for BES Cyber Systems (CIP009), 1.7 Configuration change management and vulnerability assessments (CIP010), 1.8 Information protection (CIP011) and 1.9 Declaring and responding to CIP Exceptional Circumstances.

Mapping of NIST Cybersecurity Framework v1.0 to NERC CIP version 5 & C2M2 Practices

Function	Category	Subcategory	C2M2 Practices **			NERC CIP v5
			MIL 1	MIL 2	MIL 3	
IDENTIFY (ID)	**Asset Management (AM):** The data, personnel, devices, systems, and facilities that enable the organization to achieve business purposes are identified and managed consistent with their relative importance to business objectives and the organization's risk strategy.	**ID.AM-5:** Resources (e.g., hardware, devices, data, and software) are prioritized based on their classification, criticality, and business value	ACM-1a ACM-1b	ACM-1c ACM-1d		CIP-003 R2: Each Responsible Entity for its assets identified in CIP-002-5, Requirement R1, Part R1.3, shall implement, in a manner that identifies, assesses, and corrects deficiencies, one or more documented cyber security policies that collectively address the following topics, and review and obtain CIP Senior Manager approval for those policies at least once every 15 calendar months: [Violation Risk Factor: Lower] [Time Horizon: Operations Planning] 2.1 Cyber security awareness; 2.2 Physical security controls; 2.3 Electronic access controls for external routable protocol connections and Dial-up Connectivity; and 2.4 Incident response to a Cyber Security Incident. An inventory, list, or discrete identification of low impact BES Cyber Systems or their BES Cyber Assets is not required.
IDENTIFY (ID)	**Asset Management (AM):** The data, personnel, devices, systems, and facilities that enable the organization to achieve business purposes are identified and managed consistent with their relative importance to business objectives and the organization's risk strategy.	**ID.AM-5:** Resources (e.g., hardware, devices, data, and software) are prioritized based on their classification, criticality, and business value	ACM-1a ACM-1b	ACM-1c ACM-1d		CIP-005-5 R1: Each Responsible Entity shall implement one or more documented processes that collectively include each of the applicable requirement parts in CIP-005-5 Table R1 – Electronic Security Perimeter.

			C2M2 Practices **			
Function	Category	Subcategory	MIL 1	MIL 2	MIL 3	NERC CIP v5
IDENTIFY (ID)	**Asset Management (AM):** The data, personnel, devices, systems, and facilities that enable the organization to achieve business purposes are identified and managed consistent with their relative importance to business objectives and the organization's risk strategy.	**ID.AM-5:** Resources (e.g., hardware, devices, data, and software) are prioritized based on their classification, criticality, and business value	**ACM-1a ACM-1b**	**ACM-1c ACM-1d**		CIP-009-5 R1 - 1.1: Each Responsible Entity shall have one or more documented recovery plans that collectively include each of the applicable requirement parts in CIP-009-5 Table R1: 1.1 Conditions for activation of the recovery plan(s).
IDENTIFY (ID)	**Asset Management (AM):** The data, personnel, devices, systems, and facilities that enable the organization to achieve business purposes are identified and managed consistent with their relative importance to business objectives and the organization's risk strategy.	**ID.AM-6:** Cybersecurity roles and responsibilities for the entire workforce and third-party stakeholders (e.g., suppliers, customers, partners) are established	**WM-1a WM-1b**	**WM-1c**		CIP-003-5 R1 - 1.1: Each Responsible Entity, for its high impact and medium impact BES Cyber Systems, shall review and obtain CIP Senior Manager approval at least once every 15 calendar months for one or more documented cyber security policies that collectively address the following topics: Personnel & training (CIP-004)
IDENTIFY (ID)	**Asset Management (AM):** The data, personnel, devices, systems, and facilities that enable the organization to achieve business purposes are identified and managed consistent with their relative importance to business objectives and the organization's risk strategy.	**ID.AM-6:** Cybersecurity roles and responsibilities for the entire workforce and third-party stakeholders (e.g., suppliers, customers, partners) are established	**WM-1a WM-1b**	**WM-1c**		CIP-003-5 R3: Each Responsible Entity shall identify a CIP Senior Manager by name and document any change within 30 calendar days of the change.

Mapping of NIST Cybersecurity Framework v1.0 to NERC CIP version 5 & C2M2 Practices

Function	Category	Subcategory	C2M2 Practices **			NERC CIP v5
			MIL 1	MIL 2	MIL 3	
IDENTIFY (ID)	Asset Management (AM): The data, personnel, devices, systems, and facilities that enable the organization to achieve business purposes are identified and managed consistent with their relative importance to business objectives and the organization's risk strategy.	ID.AM-6: Cybersecurity roles and responsibilities for the entire workforce and third-party stakeholders (e.g., suppliers, customers, partners) are established	WM-1a WM-1b	WM-1c		CIP-003-5 R4: The Responsible Entity shall implement, in a manner that identifies, assesses, and corrects deficiencies, a documented process to delegate authority, unless no delegations are used. Where allowed by the CIP Standards, the CIP Senior Manager may delegate authority for specific actions to a delegate or delegates. These delegations shall be documented, including the name or title of the delegate, the specific actions delegated, and the date of the delegation; approved by the CIP Senior Manager; and updated within 30 days of any change to the delegation. Delegation changes do not need to be reinstated with a change to the delegator.
IDENTIFY (ID)	Asset Management (AM): The data, personnel, devices, systems, and facilities that enable the organization to achieve business purposes are identified and managed consistent with their relative importance to business objectives and the organization's risk strategy.	ID.AM-6: Cybersecurity roles and responsibilities for the entire workforce and third-party stakeholders (e.g., suppliers, customers, partners) are established	WM-1a WM-1b	WM-1c		CIP-004-5.1 R4: Each Responsible Entity shall implement, in a manner that identifies, assesses, and corrects deficiencies, one or more documented access management programs that collectively include each of the applicable requirement parts in CIP-004-5.1 Table R4 – Access Management Program.
IDENTIFY (ID)	Business Environment (BE): The organization's mission, objectives, stakeholders, and activities are understood and prioritized; this information is used to inform cybersecurity roles, responsibilities, and risk management decisions.	ID.BE-1: The organization's role in the supply chain is identified and communicated	EDM-1b	EDM-1d	EDM-1f EDM-1g RM-1c	

Mapping of NIST Cybersecurity Framework v1.0 to NERC CIP version 5 & C2M2 Practices

Function	Category	Subcategory	C2M2 Practices **			NERC CIP v5
			MIL 1	MIL 2	MIL 3	
IDENTIFY (ID)	**Business Environment (BE):** The organization's mission, objectives, stakeholders, and activities are understood and prioritized; this information is used to inform cybersecurity roles, responsibilities, and risk management decisions.	**ID.BE-2:** The organization's place in critical infrastructure and its industry sector is identified and communicated	EDM-1b	EDM-1d CPM-1c	EDM-1f EDM-1g RM-1c	
IDENTIFY (ID)	**Business Environment (BE):** The organization's mission, objectives, stakeholders, and activities are understood and prioritized; this information is used to inform cybersecurity roles, responsibilities, and risk management decisions.	**ID.BE-3:** Priorities for organizational mission, objectives, and activities are established and communicated		RM-3b	RM-1c	
IDENTIFY (ID)	**Business Environment (BE):** The organization's mission, objectives, stakeholders, and activities are understood and prioritized; this information is used to inform cybersecurity roles, responsibilities, and risk management decisions.	**ID.BE-4:** Dependencies and critical functions for delivery of critical services are established	ACM-1a ACM-1b EDM-1a	ACM-1c ACM-1d EDM-1c EDM-1e	ACM-1e ACM-1f RM-1c EDM-1g	CIP-002-5.1 R1: Each Responsible Entity shall implement a process that considers each of the following assets for purposes of parts 1.1 through 1.3: i. Control Centers and backup Control Centers; ii. Transmission stations and substations; iii. Generation resources; iv. Systems and facilities critical to system restoration, including Blackstart Resources and Cranking Paths and initial switching requirements; v. Special Protection Systems that support the reliable operation of the Bulk Electric System; and vi. For Distribution Providers, Protection Systems specified in Applicability section 4.2.1 above.

Mapping of NIST Cybersecurity Framework v1.0 to NERC CIP version 5 & C2M2 Practices

Function	Category	Subcategory	C2M2 Practices **			NERC CIP v5
			MIL 1	MIL 2	MIL 3	
IDENTIFY (ID)	**Business Environment (BE):** The organization's mission, objectives, stakeholders, and activities are understood and prioritized; this information is used to inform cybersecurity roles, responsibilities, and risk management decisions.	**ID.BE-5:** Resilience requirements to support delivery of critical services are established	**IR-4a IR-4b IR-4c**	**IR-4e**		CIP-009-5 R1: Each Responsible Entity shall have one or more documented recovery plans that collectively include each of the applicable requirement parts in CIP-009-5 Table R1 – Recovery Plan Specifications.
IDENTIFY (ID)	**Governance (GV):** The policies, procedures, and processes to manage and monitor the organization's regulatory, legal, risk, environmental, and operational requirements are understood and inform the management of cybersecurity risk.	**ID.GV-1:** Organizational information security policy is established	**RM-1a**	**CPM-2g**	**CPM-5d RM-3e**	CIP-003-5 R1 - 1.1 to 1.9: Each Responsible Entity, for its high impact and medium impact BES Cyber Systems, shall review and obtain CIP Senior Manager approval at least once every 15 calendar months for one or more documented cyber security policies that collectively address the following topics: 1.1 Personnel & training (CIP-004) 1.2 Electronic Security Perimeters (CIP005) including interactive Remote Access, 1.3 Physical Security of BES Cyber Systems (CIP006), 1.4 System security management (CIP007), 1.5 Incident reporting and response planning (CIP008), 1.6 Recovery plans for BES Cyber Systems (CIP009), 1.7 Configuration change management and vulnerability assessments (CIP010), 1.8 Information protection (CIP011) and 1.9 Declaring and responding to CIP Exceptional Circumstances.

Mapping of NIST Cybersecurity Framework v1.0 to NERC CIP version 5 & C2M2 Practices

Function	Category	Subcategory	C2M2 Practices **			NERC CIP v5
			MIL 1	MIL 2	MIL 3	
IDENTIFY (ID)	Governance (GV): The policies, procedures, and processes to manage and monitor the organization's regulatory, legal, risk, environmental, and operational requirements are understood and inform the management of cybersecurity risk.	ID.GV-1: Organizational information security policy is established	RM-1a	CPM-2g	CPM-5d RM-3e	CIP-003-5 R2: Each Responsible Entity for its assets identified in CIP-002-5, Requirement R1, Part R1.3, shall implement, in a manner that identifies, assesses, and corrects deficiencies, one or more documented cyber security policies that collectively address the following topics, and review and obtain CIP Senior Manager approval for those policies at least once every 15 calendar months: (An inventory, list, or discrete identification of low impact BES Cyber Systems or their BES Cyber Assets is not required). (2.1) Cyber security awareness; (2.2) Physical security controls; (2.3) Electronic access controls for external routable protocol connections and Dial-up Connectivity; and (2.4) Incident response to a Cyber Security Incident.
IDENTIFY (ID)	Governance (GV): The policies, procedures, and processes to manage and monitor the organization's regulatory, legal, risk, environmental, and operational requirements are understood and inform the management of cybersecurity risk.	ID.GV-1: Organizational information security policy is established	RM-1a	CPM-2g	CPM-5d RM-3e	CIP-004-5.1 R1: Each Responsible Entity shall implement one or more documented processes that collectively include each of the applicable requirement parts in CIP-004-5.1 Table R1 – Security Awareness Program. (1.1) Security awareness that, at least once each calendar quarter, reinforces cyber security practices (which may include associated physical security practices) for the Responsible Entity's personnel who have authorized electronic or authorized unescorted physical access to BES Cyber Systems.

Mapping of NIST Cybersecurity Framework v1.0 to NERC CIP version 5 & C2M2 Practices

Function	Category	Subcategory	C2M2 Practices **			NERC CIP v5
			MIL 1	MIL 2	MIL 3	
IDENTIFY (ID)	**Governance (GV):** The policies, procedures, and processes to manage and monitor the organization's regulatory, legal, risk, environmental, and operational requirements are understood and inform the management of cybersecurity risk.	**ID.GV-1:** Organizational information security policy is established	RM-1a	CPM-2g	CPM-5d RM-3e	CIP-004-5.1 R3: Each Responsible Entity shall implement, in a manner that identifies, assesses, and corrects deficiencies, one or more documented personnel risk assessment programs to attain and retain authorized electronic or authorized unescorted physical access to BES Cyber Systems that collectively include each of the applicable requirement parts in CIP-004-5.1 Table R3 – Personnel Risk Assessment Program.
IDENTIFY (ID)	**Governance (GV):** The policies, procedures, and processes to manage and monitor the organization's regulatory, legal, risk, environmental, and operational requirements are understood and inform the management of cybersecurity risk.	**ID.GV-2:** Information security roles & responsibilities are coordinated and aligned with internal roles and external partners	WM-1a WM-1b	WM-1c WM-5b ISC-2b	WM-1f WM-1g	CIP-003-5 R3: Each Responsible Entity shall identify a CIP Senior Manager by name and document any change within 30 calendar days of the change.
IDENTIFY (ID)	**Governance (GV):** The policies, procedures, and processes to manage and monitor the organization's regulatory, legal, risk, environmental, and operational requirements are understood and inform the management of cybersecurity risk.	**ID.GV-2:** Information security roles & responsibilities are coordinated and aligned with internal roles and external partners	WM-1a WM-1b	WM-1c WM-5b ISC-2b	WM-1f WM-1g	CIP-003-5 R4: The Responsible Entity shall implement, in a manner that identifies, assesses, and corrects deficiencies, a documented process to delegate authority, unless no delegations are used. Where allowed by the CIP Standards, the CIP Senior Manager may delegate authority for specific actions to a delegate or delegates. These delegations shall be documented, including the name or title of the delegate, the specific actions delegated, and the date of the delegation; approved by the CIP Senior Manager; and updated within 30 days of any change to the delegation. Delegation changes do not need to be reinstated with a change to the delegator.

Mapping of NIST Cybersecurity Framework v1.0 to NERC CIP version 5 & C2M2 Practices

Function	Category	Subcategory	C2M2 Practices **			NERC CIP v5
			MIL 1	MIL 2	MIL 3	
IDENTIFY (ID)	Governance (GV): The policies, procedures, and processes to manage and monitor the organization's regulatory, legal, risk, environmental, and operational requirements are understood and inform the management of cybersecurity risk.	ID.GV-3: Legal and regulatory requirements regarding cybersecurity, including privacy and civil liberties obligations, are understood and managed			CPM-2k IR-3n RM-3f ACM-4f IAM-3f TVM-3f SA-4f ISC-2f IR-5f EDM-3f WM-5f	
IDENTIFY (ID)	Governance (GV): The policies, procedures, and processes to manage and monitor the organization's regulatory, legal, risk, environmental, and operational requirements are understood and inform the management of cybersecurity risk.	ID.GV-4: Governance and risk management processes address cybersecurity risks	RM-2a RM-2b	RM-3b	RM-2h RM-3e RM-1c RM-1e	
IDENTIFY (ID)	Risk Assessment (RA): The organization understands the cybersecurity risk to organizational operations (including mission, functions, image, or reputation), organizational assets, and individuals.	ID.RA-1: Asset vulnerabilities are identified and documented	TVM-2a TVM-2b TVM-2c	TVM-2d TVM-2e TVM-2f	RM-1c RM-2j TVM-2i TVM-2j TVM-2k TVM-2l TVM-2m	CIP-010-1 R3: Each Responsible Entity shall implement one or more documented processes that collectively include each of the applicable requirement parts in CIP-010 - 1 Table R3– Vulnerability Assessments.

Mapping of NIST Cybersecurity Framework v1.0 to NERC CIP version 5 & C2M2 Practices

Function	Category	Subcategory	C2M2 Practices **			NERC CIP v5
			MIL 1	MIL 2	MIL 3	
IDENTIFY (ID)	**Risk Assessment (RA):** The organization understands the cybersecurity risk to organizational operations (including mission, functions, image, or reputation), organizational assets, and individuals.	**ID.RA-1:** Asset vulnerabilities are identified and documented	TVM-2a TVM-2b TVM-2c	TVM-2d TVM-2e TVM-2f	RM-1c RM-2j TVM-2i TVM-2j TVM-2k TVM-2l TVM-2m	CIP-003-5 R1 - 1.2: Each Responsible Entity, for its high impact and medium impact BES Cyber Systems, shall review and obtain CIP Senior Manager approval at least once every 15 calendar months for one or more documented cyber security policies that collectively address the following topics: Electronic Security Perimeters (CIP-005) including Interactive Remote Access;
IDENTIFY (ID)	**Risk Assessment (RA):** The organization understands the cybersecurity risk to organizational operations (including mission, functions, image, or reputation), organizational assets, and individuals.	**ID.RA-1:** Asset vulnerabilities are identified and documented	TVM-2a TVM-2b TVM-2c	TVM-2d TVM-2e TVM-2f	RM-1c RM-2j TVM-2i TVM-2j TVM-2k TVM-2l TVM-2m	CIP-003-5 R1 - 1.4: Each Responsible Entity, for its high impact and medium impact BES Cyber Systems, shall review and obtain CIP Senior Manager approval at least once every 15 calendar months for one or more documented cyber security policies that collectively address the following topics: System security management (CIP-007);
IDENTIFY (ID)	**Risk Assessment (RA):** The organization understands the cybersecurity risk to organizational operations (including mission, functions, image, or reputation), organizational assets, and individuals.	**ID.RA-1:** Asset vulnerabilities are identified and documented	TVM-2a TVM-2b TVM-2c	TVM-2d TVM-2e TVM-2f	RM-1c RM-2j TVM-2i TVM-2j TVM-2k TVM-2l TVM-2m	CIP-003-5 R1 - 1.7: Each Responsible Entity, for its high impact and medium impact BES Cyber Systems, shall review and obtain CIP Senior Manager approval at least once every 15 calendar months for one or more documented cyber security policies that collectively address the following topics: Configuration change management and vulnerability assessments (CIP-010);

Mapping of NIST Cybersecurity Framework v1.0 to NERC CIP version 5 & C2M2 Practices

Function	Category	Subcategory	C2M2 Practices **			NERC CIP v5
			MIL 1	MIL 2	MIL 3	
IDENTIFY (ID)	**Risk Assessment (RA):** The organization understands the cybersecurity risk to organizational operations (including mission, functions, image, or reputation), organizational assets, and individuals.	**ID.RA-1:** Asset vulnerabilities are identified and documented	TVM-2a TVM-2b TVM-2c	TVM-2d TVM-2e TVM-2f	RM-1c RM-2j TVM-2i TVM-2j TVM-2k TVM-2l TVM-2m	CIP-003-5 R1 - 1.3: Each Responsible Entity, for its high impact and medium impact BES Cyber Systems, shall review and obtain CIP Senior Manager approval at least once every 15 calendar months for one or more documented cyber security policies that collectively address the following topics: Physical security of BES Cyber Systems (CIP-006);
IDENTIFY (ID)	**Risk Assessment (RA):** The organization understands the cybersecurity risk to organizational operations (including mission, functions, image, or reputation), organizational assets, and individuals.	**ID.RA-1:** Asset vulnerabilities are identified and documented	TVM-2a TVM-2b TVM-2c	TVM-2d TVM-2e TVM-2f	RM-1c RM-2j TVM-2i TVM-2j TVM-2k TVM-2l TVM-2m	CIP-007-5 R2: Each Responsible Entity shall implement, in a manner that identifies, assesses, and corrects deficiencies, one or more documented processes that collectively include each of the applicable requirement parts in CIP-007-5 Table R2 – Security Patch Management.
IDENTIFY (ID)	**Risk Assessment (RA):** The organization understands the cybersecurity risk to organizational operations (including mission, functions, image, or reputation), organizational assets, and individuals.	**ID.RA-2:** Threat and vulnerability information is received from information sharing forums and sources	TVM-1a TVM-1b TVM-2a TVM-2b			CIP-007-5 R2: Each Responsible Entity shall implement, in a manner that identifies, assesses, and corrects deficiencies, one or more documented processes that collectively include each of the applicable requirement parts in CIP-007-5 Table R2 – Security Patch Management.
IDENTIFY (ID)	**Risk Assessment (RA):** The organization understands the cybersecurity risk to organizational operations (including mission, functions, image, or reputation),	**ID.RA-2:** Threat and vulnerability information is received from information sharing forums and sources	TVM-1a TVM-1b TVM-			CIP-010-1 R3: Each Responsible Entity shall implement one or more documented processes that collectively include each of the applicable requirement parts in CIP -

58

Mapping of NIST Cybersecurity Framework v1.0 to NERC CIP version 5 & C2M2 Practices

Function	Category	Subcategory	C2M2 Practices **			NERC CIP v5
			MIL 1	MIL 2	MIL 3	
	organizational assets, and individuals.		2a TVM-2b			010 - 1 Table R3– Vulnerability Assessments.
IDENTIFY (ID)	**Risk Assessment (RA):** The organization understands the cybersecurity risk to organizational operations (including mission, functions, image, or reputation), organizational assets, and individuals.	**ID.RA-3:** Threats, both internal and external, are identified and documented	TVM-1a TVM-1b	TVM-1d TVM-1e TVM-1f	RM-1c RM-2j TVM-1i TVM-1j	CIP-007-5 R4 - 4.1: Log events at the BES Cyber System level (per BES Cyber System capability) or at the Cyber Asset level (per Cyber Asset capability) for identification of, and after-the-fact investigations of, Cyber Security Incidents that includes, as a minimum, each of the following types of events: 4.1.1. Detected successful login attempts; 4.1.2. Detected failed access attempts and failed login attempts; 4.1.3. Detected malicious code.
IDENTIFY (ID)	**Risk Assessment (RA):** The organization understands the cybersecurity risk to organizational operations (including mission, functions, image, or reputation), organizational assets, and individuals.	**ID.RA-4:** Potential business impacts and likelihoods are identified		TVM-1d TVM-1f	TVM-1i	CIP-002-5.1 R1: Each Responsible Entity shall implement a process that considers each of the following assets for purposes of parts 1.1 through 1.3: i. Control Centers and backup Control Centers; ii. Transmission stations and substations; iii. Generation resources; iv. Systems and facilities critical to system restoration, including Blackstart Resources and Cranking Paths and initial switching requirements; v. Special Protection Systems that support the reliable operation of the Bulk Electric System; and vi. For Distribution Providers, Protection Systems specified in Applicability section 4.2.1 above.

Mapping of NIST Cybersecurity Framework v1.0 to NERC CIP version 5 & C2M2 Practices

Function	Category	Subcategory	C2M2 Practices **			NERC CIP v5
			MIL 1	MIL 2	MIL 3	
IDENTIFY (ID)	**Risk Assessment (RA):** The organization understands the cybersecurity risk to organizational operations (including mission, functions, image, or reputation), organizational assets, and individuals.	**ID.RA-5:** Threats, vulnerabilities, likelihoods, and impacts are used to determine risk			RM-1c RM-2j TVM-1i TVM-2l TVM-2m	CIP-007-5 R2: Each Responsible Entity shall implement, in a manner that identifies, assesses, and corrects deficiencies, one or more documented processes that collectively include each of the applicable requirement parts in CIP-007-5 Table R2 – Security Patch Management.
IDENTIFY (ID)	**Risk Assessment (RA):** The organization understands the cybersecurity risk to organizational operations (including mission, functions, image, or reputation), organizational assets, and individuals.	**ID.RA-5:** Threats, vulnerabilities, likelihoods, and impacts are used to determine risk			RM-1c RM-2j TVM-1i TVM-2l TVM-2m	CIP-010-1 R3: Each Responsible Entity shall implement one or more documented processes that collectively include each of the applicable requirement parts in CIP-010 - 1 Table R3– Vulnerability Assessments.
IDENTIFY (ID)	**Risk Assessment (RA):** The organization understands the cybersecurity risk to organizational operations (including mission, functions, image, or reputation), organizational assets, and individuals.	**ID.RA-6:** Risk responses are identified and prioritized		RM-2e	RM-1c RM-2j TVM-1i TVM-2l IR-3m IR-4d IR-4e	CIP-007-5 R2: Each Responsible Entity shall implement, in a manner that identifies, assesses, and corrects deficiencies, one or more documented processes that collectively include each of the applicable requirement parts in CIP-007-5 Table R2 – Security Patch Management.
IDENTIFY (ID)	**Risk Assessment (RA):** The organization understands the cybersecurity risk to organizational operations (including mission, functions, image, or reputation), organizational assets, and individuals.	**ID.RA-6:** Risk responses are identified and prioritized		RM-2e	RM-1c RM-2j TVM-1i TVM-2l IR-3m IR-4d IR-4e	CIP-008-5 R1 - 1.1: Each Responsible Entity shall document one or more Cyber Security Incident response plan(s) that collectively include 1.1 One or more processes to identify, classify, and respond to Cyber Security Incidents.

Mapping of NIST Cybersecurity Framework v1.0 to NERC CIP version 5 & C2M2 Practices

Function	Category	Subcategory	C2M2 Practices **			NERC CIP v5
			MIL 1	MIL 2	MIL 3	
IDENTIFY (ID)	**Risk Assessment (RA):** The organization understands the cybersecurity risk to organizational operations (including mission, functions, image, or reputation), organizational assets, and individuals.	**ID.RA-6:** Risk responses are identified and prioritized		RM-2e	RM-1c RM-2j TVM-1i TVM-2l IR-3m IR-4d IR-4e	CIP-010-1 R3: Each Responsible Entity shall implement one or more documented processes that collectively include each of the applicable requirement parts in CIP - 010 - 1 Table R3– Vulnerability Assessments.
IDENTIFY (ID)	**Risk Management Strategy (RM):** The organization's priorities, constraints, risk tolerances, and assumptions are established and used to support operational risk decisions.	**ID.RM-1:** Risk management processes are established, managed, and agreed to by organizational stakeholders	RM-2a RM-2b	RM-1a RM-1b RM-2c RM-2d RM-2e RM-2f RM-2g RM-3a RM-3b RM-3c RM-3d	RM-1c RM-1d RM-1e RM-2h RM-2i RM-2j RM-3e RM-3f RM-3g RM-3h RM-3i	
IDENTIFY (ID)	**Risk Management Strategy (RM):** The organization's priorities, constraints, risk tolerances, and assumptions are established and used to support operational risk decisions.	**ID.RM-2:** Organizational risk tolerance is determined and clearly expressed			RM-1c RM-1e	
IDENTIFY (ID)	**Risk Management Strategy (RM):** The organization's priorities, constraints, risk tolerances, and assumptions are established and used to support operational risk decisions.	**ID.RM-3:** The organization's determination of risk tolerance is informed by their role in critical infrastructure and sector specific risk analysis		RM-1b	RM-1c	

Mapping of NIST Cybersecurity Framework v1.0 to NERC CIP version 5 & C2M2 Practices						
Function	Category	Subcategory	C2M2 Practices **			NERC CIP v5
			MIL 1	MIL 2	MIL 3	
PROTECT (PR)	**Access Control (AC):** Access to assets and associated facilities is limited to authorized users, processes, or devices, and to authorized activities and transactions.	**PR.AC-1:** Identities and credentials are managed for authorized devices and users	IAM-1a IAM-1b IAM-1c	IAM-1d IAM-1e IAM-1f	RM-1c IAM-1g	CIP-003-5 R1 - 1.1: Each Responsible Entity, for its high impact and medium impact BES Cyber Systems, shall review and obtain CIP Senior Manager approval at least once every 15 calendar months for one or more documented cyber security policies that collectively address the following topics: Personnel & training (CIP-004)
PROTECT (PR)	**Access Control (AC):** Access to assets and associated facilities is limited to authorized users, processes, or devices, and to authorized activities and transactions.	**PR.AC-1:** Identities and credentials are managed for authorized devices and users	IAM-1a IAM-1b IAM-1c	IAM-1d IAM-1e IAM-1f	RM-1c IAM-1g	CIP-003-5 R1 - 1.4: Each Responsible Entity, for its high impact and medium impact BES Cyber Systems, shall review and obtain CIP Senior Manager approval at least once every 15 calendar months for one or more documented cyber security policies that collectively address the following topics: System security management (CIP-007);
PROTECT (PR)	**Access Control (AC):** Access to assets and associated facilities is limited to authorized users, processes, or devices, and to authorized activities and transactions.	**PR.AC-1:** Identities and credentials are managed for authorized devices and users	IAM-1a IAM-1b IAM-1c	IAM-1d IAM-1e IAM-1f	RM-1c IAM-1g	CIP-003-5 R2 - 2.3: Each Responsible Entity for its assets identified in CIP-002-5, Requirement R1, Part R1.3 (i.e., low impact), shall implement, in a manner that identifies, assesses, and corrects deficiencies, one or more documented cyber security policies that collectively address the following topics, and review and obtain CIP Senior Manager approval for those policies at least once every 15 calendar months: Electronic access controls for external routable protocol connections and Dial-up Connectivity
PROTECT (PR)	**Access Control (AC):** Access to assets and associated facilities is limited to authorized users, processes, or devices, and to authorized activities and transactions.	**PR.AC-1:** Identities and credentials are managed for authorized devices and users	IAM-1a IAM-1b IAM-1c	IAM-1d IAM-1e IAM-1f	RM-1c IAM-1g	CIP-004-5.1 R4: Each Responsible Entity shall implement, in a manner that identifies, assesses, and corrects deficiencies, one or more documented access management programs that collectively include each of the applicable

Mapping of NIST Cybersecurity Framework v1.0 to NERC CIP version 5 & C2M2 Practices

Function	Category	Subcategory	C2M2 Practices **			NERC CIP v5
			MIL 1	MIL 2	MIL 3	
						requirement parts in CIP-004-5.1 Table R4 – Access Management Program.
PROTECT (PR)	**Access Control (AC):** Access to assets and associated facilities is limited to authorized users, processes, or devices, and to authorized activities and transactions.	**PR.AC-1:** Identities and credentials are managed for authorized devices and users	IAM-1a IAM-1b IAM-1c	IAM-1d IAM-1e IAM-1f	RM-1c IAM-1g	CIP-004-5.1 R5: Each Responsible Entity shall implement, in a manner that identifies, assesses, and corrects deficiencies, one or more documented access revocation programs that collectively include each of the applicable requirement parts in CIP-004-5.1 Table R5 – Access Revocation.
PROTECT (PR)	**Access Control (AC):** Access to assets and associated facilities is limited to authorized users, processes, or devices, and to authorized activities and transactions.	**PR.AC-1:** Identities and credentials are managed for authorized devices and users	IAM-1a IAM-1b IAM-1c	IAM-1d IAM-1e IAM-1f	RM-1c IAM-1g	CIP-007-5 R5: Each Responsible Entity shall implement, in a manner that identifies, assesses, and corrects deficiencies, one or more documented processes that collectively include each of the applicable requirement parts in CIP-007-5 Table R5 – System Access Controls.
PROTECT (PR)	**Access Control (AC):** Access to assets and associated facilities is limited to authorized users, processes, or devices, and to authorized activities and transactions.	**PR.AC-2:** Physical access to assets is managed and protected	IAM-2a IAM-2b IAM-2c	IAM-2d IAM-2e IAM-2f	IAM-2g	CIP-003-5 R1 - 1.1: Each Responsible Entity, for its high impact and medium impact BES Cyber Systems, shall review and obtain CIP Senior Manager approval at least once every 15 calendar months for one or more documented cyber security policies that collectively address the following topics: Personnel & training (CIP-004)
PROTECT (PR)	**Access Control (AC):** Access to assets and associated facilities is limited to authorized users, processes, or devices, and to authorized activities and transactions.	**PR.AC-2:** Physical access to assets is managed and protected	IAM-2a IAM-2b IAM-2c	IAM-2d IAM-2e IAM-2f	IAM-2g	CIP-003-5 R1 - 1.3: Each Responsible Entity, for its high impact and medium impact BES Cyber Systems, shall review and obtain CIP Senior Manager approval at least once every 15 calendar months for one or more documented cyber security

Mapping of NIST Cybersecurity Framework v1.0 to NERC CIP version 5 & C2M2 Practices

Function	Category	Subcategory	C2M2 Practices **			NERC CIP v5
			MIL 1	MIL 2	MIL 3	
						policies that collectively address the following topics: Physical security of BES Cyber Systems (CIP-006);
PROTECT (PR)	**Access Control (AC):** Access to assets and associated facilities is limited to authorized users, processes, or devices, and to authorized activities and transactions.	**PR.AC-2:** Physical access to assets is managed and protected	IAM-2a IAM-2b IAM-2c	IAM-2d IAM-2e IAM-2f	IAM-2g	CIP-003-5 R2 - 2.2: Each Responsible Entity for its assets identified in CIP-002-5, Requirement R1, Part R1.3, shall implement, in a manner that identifies, assesses, and corrects deficiencies, one or more documented cyber security policies that collectively address the following topics, and review and obtain CIP Senior Manager approval for those policies at least once every 15 calendar months: Physical security controls;
PROTECT (PR)	**Access Control (AC):** Access to assets and associated facilities is limited to authorized users, processes, or devices, and to authorized activities and transactions.	**PR.AC-2:** Physical access to assets is managed and protected	IAM-2a IAM-2b IAM-2c	IAM-2d IAM-2e IAM-2f	IAM-2g	CIP-004-5.1 R4: Each Responsible Entity shall implement, in a manner that identifies, assesses, and corrects deficiencies, one or more documented access management programs that collectively include each of the applicable requirement parts in CIP-004-5.1 Table R4 – Access Management Program.
PROTECT (PR)	**Access Control (AC):** Access to assets and associated facilities is limited to authorized users, processes, or devices, and to authorized activities and transactions.	**PR.AC-2:** Physical access to assets is managed and protected	IAM-2a IAM-2b IAM-2c	IAM-2d IAM-2e IAM-2f	IAM-2g	CIP-004-5.1 R5: Each Responsible Entity shall implement, in a manner that identifies, assesses, and corrects deficiencies, one or more documented access revocation programs that collectively include each of the applicable requirement parts in CIP-004-5.1 Table R5 – Access Revocation.

Mapping of NIST Cybersecurity Framework v1.0 to NERC CIP version 5 & C2M2 Practices

Function	Category	Subcategory	C2M2 Practices **			NERC CIP v5
			MIL 1	MIL 2	MIL 3	
PROTECT (PR)	**Access Control (AC):** Access to assets and associated facilities is limited to authorized users, processes, or devices, and to authorized activities and transactions.	**PR.AC-2:** Physical access to assets is managed and protected	IAM-2a IAM-2b IAM-2c	IAM-2d IAM-2e IAM-2f	IAM-2g	CIP-006-5 R1: Each Responsible Entity shall implement, in a manner that identifies, assesses, and corrects deficiencies, one or more documented physical security plans that collectively include all of the applicable requirement parts in CIP-006-5 Table R1 – Physical Security Plan.
PROTECT (PR)	**Access Control (AC):** Access to assets and associated facilities is limited to authorized users, processes, or devices, and to authorized activities and transactions.	**PR.AC-2:** Physical access to assets is managed and protected	IAM-2a IAM-2b IAM-2c	IAM-2d IAM-2e IAM-2f	IAM-2g	CIP-006-5 R2: Each Responsible Entity shall implement, in a manner that identifies, assesses, and corrects deficiencies, one or more documented visitor control programs that include each of the applicable requirement parts in CIP-006-5 Table R2 – Visitor Control Program.
PROTECT (PR)	**Access Control (AC):** Access to assets and associated facilities is limited to authorized users, processes, or devices, and to authorized activities and transactions.	**PR.AC-3:** Remote access is managed	IAM-2a IAM-2b IAM-2c	IAM-2d IAM-2e IAM-2f	IAM-2g	CIP-003-5 R1 - 1.1: Each Responsible Entity, for its high impact and medium impact BES Cyber Systems, shall review and obtain CIP Senior Manager approval at least once every 15 calendar months for one or more documented cyber security policies that collectively address the following topics: Personnel & training (CIP-004)
PROTECT (PR)	**Access Control (AC):** Access to assets and associated facilities is limited to authorized users, processes, or devices, and to authorized activities and transactions.	**PR.AC-3:** Remote access is managed	IAM-2a IAM-2b IAM-2c	IAM-2d IAM-2e IAM-2f	IAM-2g	CIP-003-5 R1 - 1.2: Each Responsible Entity, for its high impact and medium impact BES Cyber Systems, shall review and obtain CIP Senior Manager approval at least once every 15 calendar months for one or more documented cyber security policies that collectively address the following topics: Electronic Security Perimeters (CIP-005) including Interactive Remote Access;

Mapping of NIST Cybersecurity Framework v1.0 to NERC CIP version 5 & C2M2 Practices

Function	Category	Subcategory	C2M2 Practices **			NERC CIP v5
			MIL 1	MIL 2	MIL 3	
PROTECT (PR)	Access Control (AC): Access to assets and associated facilities is limited to authorized users, processes, or devices, and to authorized activities and transactions.	PR.AC-3: Remote access is managed	IAM-2a IAM-2b IAM-2c	IAM-2d IAM-2e IAM-2f	IAM-2g	CIP-003-5 R2 - 2.3: Each Responsible Entity for its assets identified in CIP-002-5, Requirement R1, Part R1.3 (i.e, low impact), shall implement, in a manner that identifies, assesses, and corrects deficiencies, one or more documented cyber security policies that collectively address the following topics, and review and obtain CIP Senior Manager approval for those policies at least once every 15 calendar months: Electronic access controls for external routable protocol connections and Dial-up Connectivity
PROTECT (PR)	Access Control (AC): Access to assets and associated facilities is limited to authorized users, processes, or devices, and to authorized activities and transactions.	PR.AC-3: Remote access is managed	IAM-2a IAM-2b IAM-2c	IAM-2d IAM-2e IAM-2f	IAM-2g	CIP-004-5.1 R4: Each Responsible Entity shall implement, in a manner that identifies, assesses, and corrects deficiencies, one or more documented access management programs that collectively include each of the applicable requirement parts in CIP-004-5.1 Table R4 – Access Management Program.
PROTECT (PR)	Access Control (AC): Access to assets and associated facilities is limited to authorized users, processes, or devices, and to authorized activities and transactions.	PR.AC-3: Remote access is managed	IAM-2a IAM-2b IAM-2c	IAM-2d IAM-2e IAM-2f	IAM-2g	CIP-004-5.1 R5: Each Responsible Entity shall implement, in a manner that identifies, assesses, and corrects deficiencies, one or more documented access revocation programs that collectively include each of the applicable requirement parts in CIP-004-5.1 Table R5 – Access Revocation.
PROTECT (PR)	Access Control (AC): Access to assets and associated facilities is limited to authorized users, processes, or devices, and to authorized activities and transactions.	PR.AC-3: Remote access is managed	IAM-2a IAM-2b IAM-2c	IAM-2d IAM-2e IAM-2f	IAM-2g	CIP-005-5 R1: Each Responsible Entity shall implement one or more documented processes that collectively include each of the applicable requirement parts in CIP-005-5 Table R1 – Electronic Security Perimeter.

Mapping of NIST Cybersecurity Framework v1.0 to NERC CIP version 5 & C2M2 Practices

Function	Category	Subcategory	C2M2 Practices **			NERC CIP v5
			MIL 1	MIL 2	MIL 3	
PROTECT (PR)	**Access Control (AC):** Access to assets and associated facilities is limited to authorized users, processes, or devices, and to authorized activities and transactions.	**PR.AC-3:** Remote access is managed	IAM-2a IAM-2b IAM-2c	IAM-2d IAM-2e IAM-2f	IAM-2g	CIP-005-5 R2: Each Responsible Entity allowing Interactive Remote Access to BES Cyber Systems shall implement one or more documented processes that collectively include the applicable requirement parts, where technically feasible, in CIP-005-5 Table R2 – Interactive Remote Access Management.
PROTECT (PR)	**Access Control (AC):** Access to assets and associated facilities is limited to authorized users, processes, or devices, and to authorized activities and transactions.	**PR.AC-4:** Access permissions are managed, incorporating the principles of least privilege and separation of duties		IAM-2d		CIP-003-5 R1 - 1.4: Each Responsible Entity, for its high impact and medium impact BES Cyber Systems, shall review and obtain CIP Senior Manager approval at least once every 15 calendar months for one or more documented cyber security policies that collectively address the following topics: System security management (CIP-007);
PROTECT (PR)	**Access Control (AC):** Access to assets and associated facilities is limited to authorized users, processes, or devices, and to authorized activities and transactions.	**PR.AC-4:** Access permissions are managed, incorporating the principles of least privilege and separation of duties		IAM-2d		CIP-003-5 R1 - 1.8: Each Responsible Entity, for its high impact and medium impact BES Cyber Systems, shall review and obtain CIP Senior Manager approval at least once every 15 calendar months for one or more documented cyber security policies that collectively address the following topics: Information protection (CIP-011);
PROTECT (PR)	**Access Control (AC):** Access to assets and associated facilities is limited to authorized users, processes, or devices, and to authorized activities and transactions.	**PR.AC-4:** Access permissions are managed, incorporating the principles of least privilege and separation of duties		IAM-2d		CIP-004-5.1 R4: Each Responsible Entity shall implement, in a manner that identifies, assesses, and corrects deficiencies, one or more documented access management programs that collectively include each of the applicable requirement parts in CIP-004-5.1 Table R4 – Access Management Program.

			C2M2 Practices **			
Function	Category	Subcategory	MIL 1	MIL 2	MIL 3	NERC CIP v5
PROTECT (PR)	**Access Control (AC):** Access to assets and associated facilities is limited to authorized users, processes, or devices, and to authorized activities and transactions.	**PR.AC-4:** Access permissions are managed, incorporating the principles of least privilege and separation of duties		IAM-2d		CIP-004-5.1 R5: Each Responsible Entity shall implement, in a manner that identifies, assesses, and corrects deficiencies, one or more documented access revocation programs that collectively include each of the applicable requirement parts in CIP-004-5.1 Table R5 – Access Revocation.
PROTECT (PR)	**Access Control (AC):** Access to assets and associated facilities is limited to authorized users, processes, or devices, and to authorized activities and transactions.	**PR.AC-4:** Access permissions are managed, incorporating the principles of least privilege and separation of duties		IAM-2d		CIP-007-5 R5: Each Responsible Entity shall implement, in a manner that identifies, assesses, and corrects deficiencies, one or more documented processes that collectively include each of the applicable requirement parts in CIP-007-5 Table R5 – System Access Controls.
PROTECT (PR)	**Access Control (AC):** Access to assets and associated facilities is limited to authorized users, processes, or devices, and to authorized activities and transactions.	**PR.AC-5:** Network integrity is protected, incorporating network segregation where appropriate	CPM-3a	CPM-3b CPM-3c	CPM-3d	CIP-003-5 R1 - 1.2: Each Responsible Entity, for its high impact and medium impact BES Cyber Systems, shall review and obtain CIP Senior Manager approval at least once every 15 calendar months for one or more documented cyber security policies that collectively address the following topics: Electronic Security Perimeters (CIP-005) including Interactive Remote Access;
PROTECT (PR)	**Access Control (AC):** Access to assets and associated facilities is limited to authorized users, processes, or devices, and to authorized activities and transactions.	**PR.AC-5:** Network integrity is protected, incorporating network segregation where appropriate	CPM-3a	CPM-3b CPM-3c	CPM-3d	CIP-003-5 R1 - 1.8: Each Responsible Entity, for its high impact and medium impact BES Cyber Systems, shall review and obtain CIP Senior Manager approval at least once every 15 calendar months for one or more documented cyber security policies that collectively address the following topics: Information protection (CIP-011);

Mapping of NIST Cybersecurity Framework v1.0 to NERC CIP version 5 & C2M2 Practices

Mapping of NIST Cybersecurity Framework v1.0 to NERC CIP version 5 & C2M2 Practices

Function	Category	Subcategory	C2M2 Practices **			NERC CIP v5
			MIL 1	MIL 2	MIL 3	
PROTECT (PR)	**Access Control (AC):** Access to assets and associated facilities is limited to authorized users, processes, or devices, and to authorized activities and transactions.	**PR.AC-5:** Network integrity is protected, incorporating network segregation where appropriate	CPM-3a	CPM-3b CPM-3c	CPM-3d	CIP-005-5 R1: Each Responsible Entity shall implement one or more documented processes that collectively include each of the applicable requirement parts in CIP-005-5 Table R1 – Electronic Security Perimeter.
PROTECT (PR)	**Access Control (AC):** Access to assets and associated facilities is limited to authorized users, processes, or devices, and to authorized activities and transactions.	**PR.AC-5:** Network integrity is protected, incorporating network segregation where appropriate	CPM-3a	CPM-3b CPM-3c	CPM-3d	CIP-007-5 R1: Each Responsible Entity shall implement, in a manner that identifies, assesses, and corrects deficiencies, one or more documented processes that collectively include each of the applicable requirement parts in CIP-007-5 Table R1 – Ports and Services.
PROTECT (PR)	**Awareness and Training (AT):** The organization's personnel and partners are provided cybersecurity awareness education and are adequately trained to perform their information security-related duties and responsibilities consistent with related policies, procedures, and agreements.	**PR.AT-1:** All users are informed and trained	WM-3a	WM-3b WM-3c WM-3d	WM-3e WM-3f WM-3g WM-3h WM-3i	CIP-003-5 R1 - 1.1 to 1.9: Each Responsible Entity, for its high impact and medium impact BES Cyber Systems, shall review and obtain CIP Senior Manager approval at least once every 15 calendar months for one or more documented cyber security policies that collectively address the following topics: 1.1 Personnel & training (CIP-004) 1.2 Electronic Security Perimeters (CIP005) including interactive Remote Access, 1.3 Physical Security of BES Cyber Systems (CIP006), 1.4 System security management (CIP007), 1.5 Incident reporting and response planning (CIP008), 1.6 Recovery plans for BES Cyber Systems (CIP009), 1.7 Configuration change management and vulnerability assessments (CIP010), 1.8 Information protection (CIP011) and 1.9 Declaring and responding to CIP Exceptional Circumstances.

Mapping of NIST Cybersecurity Framework v1.0 to NERC CIP version 5 & C2M2 Practices						
Function	Category	Subcategory	C2M2 Practices **			NERC CIP v5
			MIL 1	MIL 2	MIL 3	
PROTECT (PR)	**Awareness and Training (AT):** The organization's personnel and partners are provided cybersecurity awareness education and are adequately trained to perform their information security-related duties and responsibilities consistent with related policies, procedures, and agreements.	**PR.AT-1:** All users are informed and trained	WM-3a	WM-3b WM-3c WM-3d	WM-3e WM-3f WM-3g WM-3h WM-3i	CIP-003-5 R2 - 2.1: Each Responsible Entity for its assets identified in CIP-002-5, Requirement R1, Part R1.3, shall implement, in a manner that identifies, assesses, and corrects deficiencies, one or more documented cyber security policies that collectively address the following topics, and review and obtain CIP Senior Manager approval for those policies at least once every 15 calendar months: (An inventory, list, or discrete identification of low impact BES Cyber Systems or their BES Cyber Assets is not required). Cyber security awareness;
PROTECT (PR)	**Awareness and Training (AT):** The organization's personnel and partners are provided cybersecurity awareness education and are adequately trained to perform their information security-related duties and responsibilities consistent with related policies, procedures, and agreements.	**PR.AT-1:** All users are informed and trained	WM-3a	WM-3b WM-3c WM-3d	WM-3e WM-3f WM-3g WM-3h WM-3i	CIP-004-5.1 R1: Each Responsible Entity shall implement one or more documented processes that collectively include each of the applicable requirement parts in CIP-004-5.1 Table R1 – Security Awareness Program. (1.1) Security awareness that, at least once each calendar quarter, reinforces cyber security practices (which may include associated physical security practices) for the Responsible Entity's personnel who have authorized electronic or authorized unescorted physical access to BES Cyber Systems.
PROTECT (PR)	**Awareness and Training (AT):** The organization's personnel and partners are provided cybersecurity awareness education and are adequately trained to perform their information security-related duties and responsibilities consistent with related policies, procedures, and agreements.	**PR.AT-1:** All users are informed and trained	WM-3a	WM-3b WM-3c WM-3d	WM-3e WM-3f WM-3g WM-3h WM-3i	CIP-004-5.1 R2: Each Responsible Entity shall implement, in a manner that identifies, assesses, and corrects deficiencies, a cyber security training program(s) appropriate to individual roles, functions, or responsibilities that collectively includes each of the applicable requirement parts in CIP-004-5.1 Table R2 – Cyber Security Training Program.

CYBERSECURITY FRAMEWORK
SMART GRID PROFILE

Mapping of NIST Cybersecurity Framework v1.0 to NERC CIP version 5 & C2M2 Practices

Function	Category	Subcategory	C2M2 Practices **			NERC CIP v5
			MIL 1	MIL 2	MIL 3	
PROTECT (PR)	**Awareness and Training (AT):** The organization's personnel and partners are provided cybersecurity awareness education and are adequately trained to perform their information security-related duties and responsibilities consistent with related policies, procedures, and agreements.	**PR.AT-2:** Privileged users understand roles & responsibilities.	WM-1a WM-1b	WM-1c WM-1d	WM-1e WM-1f WM-1g	CIP-003-5 R1 - 1.1 to 1.9: Each Responsible Entity, for its high impact and medium impact BES Cyber Systems, shall review and obtain CIP Senior Manager approval at least once every 15 calendar months for one or more documented cyber security policies that collectively address the following topics: 1.1 Personnel & training (CIP-004) 1.2 Electronic Security Perimeters (CIP005) including interactive Remote Access, 1.3 Physical Security of BES Cyber Systems (CIP006), 1.4 System security management (CIP007), 1.5 Incident reporting and response planning (CIP008), 1.6 Recovery plans for BES Cyber Systems (CIP009), 1.7 Configuration change management and vulnerability assessments (CIP010), 1.8 Information protection (CIP011) and 1.9 Declaring and responding to CIP Exceptional Circumstances.
PROTECT (PR)	**Awareness and Training (AT):** The organization's personnel and partners are provided cybersecurity awareness education and are adequately trained to perform their information security-related duties and responsibilities consistent with related policies, procedures, and agreements.	**PR.AT-2:** Privileged users understand roles & responsibilities.	WM-1a WM-1b	WM-1c WM-1d	WM-1e WM-1f WM-1g	CIP-003-5 R2 - 2.1: Each Responsible Entity for its assets identified in CIP-002-5, Requirement R1, Part R1.3, shall implement, in a manner that identifies, assesses, and corrects deficiencies, one or more documented cyber security policies that collectively address the following topics, and review and obtain CIP Senior Manager approval for those policies at least once every 15 calendar months: (An inventory, list, or discrete identification of low impact BES Cyber Systems or their BES Cyber Assets is not required). Cyber security awareness;

Mapping of NIST Cybersecurity Framework v1.0 to NERC CIP version 5 & C2M2 Practices

Function	Category	Subcategory	C2M2 Practices **			NERC CIP v5
			MIL 1	MIL 2	MIL 3	
PROTECT (PR)	**Awareness and Training (AT):** The organization's personnel and partners are provided cybersecurity awareness education and are adequately trained to perform their information security-related duties and responsibilities consistent with related policies, procedures, and agreements.	**PR.AT-2:** Privileged users understand roles & responsibilities.	WM-1a WM-1b	WM-1c WM-1d	WM-1e WM-1f WM-1g	CIP-004-5.1 R1: Each Responsible Entity shall implement one or more documented processes that collectively include each of the applicable requirement parts in CIP-004-5.1 Table R1 – Security Awareness Program. (1.1) Security awareness that, at least once each calendar quarter, reinforces cyber security practices (which may include associated physical security practices) for the Responsible Entity's personnel who have authorized electronic or authorized unescorted physical access to BES Cyber Systems.
PROTECT (PR)	**Awareness and Training (AT):** The organization's personnel and partners are provided cybersecurity awareness education and are adequately trained to perform their information security-related duties and responsibilities consistent with related policies, procedures, and agreements.	**PR.AT-2:** Privileged users understand roles & responsibilities.	WM-1a WM-1b	WM-1c WM-1d	WM-1e WM-1f WM-1g	CIP-004-5.1 R2: Each Responsible Entity shall implement, in a manner that identifies, assesses, and corrects deficiencies, a cyber security training program(s) appropriate to individual roles, functions, or responsibilities that collectively includes each of the applicable requirement parts in CIP-004-5.1 Table R2 – Cyber Security Training Program.
PROTECT (PR)	**Awareness and Training (AT):** The organization's personnel and partners are provided cybersecurity awareness education and are adequately trained to perform their information security-related duties and responsibilities consistent with related policies, procedures, and agreements.	**PR.AT-3:** Third-party stakeholders (e.g., suppliers, customers, partners) understand roles & responsibilities	WM-1a WM-1b	WM-1c WM-1d	WM-1e WM-1f WM-1g	CIP-003-5 R1 - 1.1 to 1.9: Each Responsible Entity, for its high impact and medium impact BES Cyber Systems, shall review and obtain CIP Senior Manager approval at least once every 15 calendar months for one or more documented cyber security policies that collectively address the following topics: 1.1 Personnel & training (CIP-004) 1.2 Electronic Security Perimeters (CIP005) including interactive Remote Access, 1.3 Physical Security of BES Cyber Systems (CIP006), 1.4 System security management (CIP007), 1.5 Incident reporting and response planning

72

Mapping of NIST Cybersecurity Framework v1.0 to NERC CIP version 5 & C2M2 Practices

Function	Category	Subcategory	C2M2 Practices **			NERC CIP v5
			MIL 1	MIL 2	MIL 3	
						(CIP008), 1.6 Recovery plans for BES Cyber Systems (CIP009), 1.7 Configuration change management and vulnerability assessments (CIP010), 1.8 Information protection (CIP011) and 1.9 Declaring and responding to CIP Exceptional Circumstances.
PROTECT (PR)	Awareness and Training (AT): The organization's personnel and partners are provided cybersecurity awareness education and are adequately trained to perform their information security-related duties and responsibilities consistent with related policies, procedures, and agreements.	PR.AT-3: Third-party stakeholders (e.g., suppliers, customers, partners) understand roles & responsibilities	WM-1a WM-1b	WM-1c WM-1d	WM-1e WM-1f WM-1g	CIP-003-5 R2 - 2.1: Each Responsible Entity for its assets identified in CIP-002-5, Requirement R1, Part R1.3, shall implement, in a manner that identifies, assesses, and corrects deficiencies, one or more documented cyber security policies that collectively address the following topics, and review and obtain CIP Senior Manager approval for those policies at least once every 15 calendar months: (An inventory, list, or discrete identification of low impact BES Cyber Systems or their BES Cyber Assets is not required). Cyber security awareness;
PROTECT (PR)	Awareness and Training (AT): The organization's personnel and partners are provided cybersecurity awareness education and are adequately trained to perform their information security-related duties and responsibilities consistent with	PR.AT-3: Third-party stakeholders (e.g., suppliers, customers, partners) understand roles & responsibilities	WM-1a WM-1b	WM-1c WM-1d	WM-1e WM-1f WM-1g	CIP-004-5.1 R1: Each Responsible Entity shall implement one or more documented processes that collectively include each of the applicable requirement parts in CIP-004-5.1 Table R1 – Security Awareness Program. (1.1) Security awareness that, at least once each calendar quarter, reinforces cyber security practices (which may include associated physical security

Mapping of NIST Cybersecurity Framework v1.0 to NERC CIP version 5 & C2M2 Practices

Function	Category	Subcategory	C2M2 Practices **			NERC CIP v5
			MIL 1	MIL 2	MIL 3	
	related policies, procedures, and agreements.					practices) for the Responsible Entity's personnel who have authorized electronic or authorized unescorted physical access to BES Cyber Systems.
PROTECT (PR)	**Awareness and Training (AT):** The organization's personnel and partners are provided cybersecurity awareness education and are adequately trained to perform their information security-related duties and responsibilities consistent with related policies, procedures, and agreements.	**PR.AT-3:** Third-party stakeholders (e.g., suppliers, customers, partners) understand roles & responsibilities	WM-1a WM-1b	WM-1c WM-1d	WM-1e WM-1f WM-1g	CIP-004-5.1 R2: Each Responsible Entity shall implement, in a manner that identifies, assesses, and corrects deficiencies, a cyber security training program(s) appropriate to individual roles, functions, or responsibilities that collectively includes each of the applicable requirement parts in CIP-004-5.1 Table R2 – Cyber Security Training Program.
PROTECT (PR)	**Awareness and Training (AT):** The organization's personnel and partners are provided cybersecurity awareness education and are adequately trained to perform their information security-related duties and responsibilities consistent with related policies, procedures, and agreements.	**PR.AT-4:** Senior executives understand roles & responsibilities	WM-1a WM-1b	WM-1c WM-1d	WM-1e WM-1f WM-1g	CIP-003-5 R1 - 1.1 to 1.9: Each Responsible Entity, for its high impact and medium impact BES Cyber Systems, shall review and obtain CIP Senior Manager approval at least once every 15 calendar months for one or more documented cyber security policies that collectively address the following topics: 1.1 Personnel & training (CIP-004) 1.2 Electronic Security Perimeters (CIP005) including interactive Remote Access, 1.3 Physical Security of BES Cyber Systems (CIP006), 1.4 System security management (CIP007), 1.5 Incident reporting and response planning (CIP008), 1.6 Recovery plans for BES Cyber Systems (CIP009), 1.7 Configuration change management and vulnerability assessments (CIP010), 1.8

74

Mapping of NIST Cybersecurity Framework v1.0 to NERC CIP version 5 & C2M2 Practices

Function	Category	Subcategory	C2M2 Practices **			NERC CIP v5
			MIL 1	MIL 2	MIL 3	
						Information protection (CIP011) and 1.9 Declaring and responding to CIP Exceptional Circumstances.
PROTECT (PR)	**Awareness and Training (AT):** The organization's personnel and partners are provided cybersecurity awareness education and are adequately trained to perform their information security-related duties and responsibilities consistent with related policies, procedures, and agreements.	**PR.AT-4:** Senior executives understand roles & responsibilities	**WM-1a** **WM-1b**	**WM-1c** **WM-1d**	**WM-1e** **WM-1f** **WM-1g**	CIP-003-5 R2 - 2.1: Each Responsible Entity for its assets identified in CIP-002-5, Requirement R1, Part R1.3, shall implement, in a manner that identifies, assesses, and corrects deficiencies, one or more documented cyber security policies that collectively address the following topics, and review and obtain CIP Senior Manager approval for those policies at least once every 15 calendar months: (An inventory, list, or discrete identification of low impact BES Cyber Systems or their BES Cyber Assets is not required). Cyber security awareness;

Mapping of NIST Cybersecurity Framework v1.0 to NERC CIP version 5 & C2M2 Practices

Function	Category	Subcategory	C2M2 Practices **			NERC CIP v5
			MIL 1	MIL 2	MIL 3	
PROTECT (PR)	**Awareness and Training (AT):** The organization's personnel and partners are provided cybersecurity awareness education and are adequately trained to perform their information security-related duties and responsibilities consistent with related policies, procedures, and agreements.	**PR.AT-4:** Senior executives understand roles & responsibilities	WM-1a WM-1b	WM-1c WM-1d	WM-1e WM-1f WM-1g	CIP-003-5 R4: The Responsible Entity shall implement, in a manner that identifies, assesses, and corrects deficiencies, a documented process to delegate authority, unless no delegations are used. Where allowed by the CIP Standards, the CIP Senior Manager may delegate authority for specific actions to a delegate or delegates. These delegations shall be documented, including the name or title of the delegate, the specific actions delegated, and the date of the delegation; approved by the CIP Senior Manager; and updated within 30 days of any change to the delegation. Delegation changes do not need to be reinstated with a change to the delegator.
PROTECT (PR)	**Awareness and Training (AT):** The organization's personnel and partners are provided cybersecurity awareness education and are adequately trained to perform their information security-related duties and responsibilities consistent with related policies, procedures, and agreements.	**PR.AT-4:** Senior executives understand roles & responsibilities	WM-1a WM-1b	WM-1c WM-1d	WM-1e WM-1f WM-1g	CIP-004-5.1 R1: Each Responsible Entity shall implement one or more documented processes that collectively include each of the applicable requirement parts in CIP-004-5.1 Table R1 – Security Awareness Program. (1.1) Security awareness that, at least once each calendar quarter, reinforces cyber security practices (which may include associated physical security practices) for the Responsible Entity's personnel who have authorized electronic or authorized unescorted physical access to BES Cyber Systems.
PROTECT (PR)	**Awareness and Training (AT):** The organization's personnel and partners are provided cybersecurity awareness education and are adequately trained to perform their information security-related duties and	**PR.AT-4:** Senior executives understand roles & responsibilities	WM-1a WM-1b	WM-1c WM-1d	WM-1e WM-1f WM-1g	CIP-004-5.1 R2: Each Responsible Entity shall implement, in a manner that identifies, assesses, and corrects deficiencies, a cyber security training program(s) appropriate to individual roles, functions, or responsibilities that collectively includes each of the applicable

	Mapping of NIST Cybersecurity Framework v1.0 to NERC CIP version 5 & C2M2 Practices					
			C2M2 Practices **			NERC CIP v5
Function	Category	Subcategory	MIL 1	MIL 2	MIL 3	
	responsibilities consistent with related policies, procedures, and agreements.					requirement parts in CIP-004-5.1 Table R2 – Cyber Security Training Program.
PROTECT (PR)	**Awareness and Training (AT):** The organization's personnel and partners are provided cybersecurity awareness education and are adequately trained to perform their information security-related duties and responsibilities consistent with related policies, procedures, and agreements.	**PR.AT-5:** Physical and information security personnel understand roles & responsibilities	WM-1a WM-1b	WM-1c WM-1d	WM-1e WM-1f WM-1g	CIP-003-5 R1 - 1.1 to 1.9: Each Responsible Entity, for its high impact and medium impact BES Cyber Systems, shall review and obtain CIP Senior Manager approval at least once every 15 calendar months for one or more documented cyber security policies that collectively address the following topics: 1.1 Personnel & training (CIP-004) 1.2 Electronic Security Perimeters (CIP005) including interactive Remote Access, 1.3 Physical Security of BES Cyber Systems (CIP006), 1.4 System security management (CIP007), 1.5 Incident reporting and response planning (CIP008), 1.6 Recovery plans for BES Cyber Systems (CIP009), 1.7 Configuration change management and vulnerability assessments (CIP010), 1.8 Information protection (CIP011) and 1.9 Declaring and responding to CIP Exceptional Circumstances.

				C2M2 Practices **			
Mapping of NIST Cybersecurity Framework v1.0 to NERC CIP version 5 & C2M2 Practices							
Function	**Category**	**Subcategory**	**MIL 1**	**MIL 2**	**MIL 3**	**NERC CIP v5**	
PROTECT (PR)	**Awareness and Training (AT):** The organization's personnel and partners are provided cybersecurity awareness education and are adequately trained to perform their information security-related duties and responsibilities consistent with related policies, procedures, and agreements.	**PR.AT-5:** Physical and information security personnel understand roles & responsibilities	WM-1a WM-1b	WM-1c WM-1d	WM-1e WM-1f WM-1g	CIP-003-5 R2 - 2.1: Each Responsible Entity for its assets identified in CIP-002-5, Requirement R1, Part R1.3, shall implement, in a manner that identifies, assesses, and corrects deficiencies, one or more documented cyber security policies that collectively address the following topics, and review and obtain CIP Senior Manager approval for those policies at least once every 15 calendar months: (An inventory, list, or discrete identification of low impact BES Cyber Systems or their BES Cyber Assets is not required). Cyber security awareness;	
PROTECT (PR)	**Awareness and Training (AT):** The organization's personnel and partners are provided cybersecurity awareness education and are adequately trained to perform their information security-related duties and responsibilities consistent with related policies, procedures, and agreements.	**PR.AT-5:** Physical and information security personnel understand roles & responsibilities	WM-1a WM-1b	WM-1c WM-1d	WM-1e WM-1f WM-1g	CIP-004-5.1 R1: Each Responsible Entity shall implement one or more documented processes that collectively include each of the applicable requirement parts in CIP-004-5.1 Table R1 – Security Awareness Program. (1.1) Security awareness that, at least once each calendar quarter, reinforces cyber security practices (which may include associated physical security practices) for the Responsible Entity's personnel who have authorized electronic or authorized unescorted physical access to BES Cyber Systems.	
PROTECT (PR)	**Awareness and Training (AT):** The organization's personnel and partners are provided cybersecurity awareness education and are adequately trained to perform their information security-related duties and responsibilities consistent with related policies, procedures, and agreements.	**PR.AT-5:** Physical and information security personnel understand roles & responsibilities	WM-1a WM-1b	WM-1c WM-1d	WM-1e WM-1f WM-1g	CIP-004-5.1 R2: Each Responsible Entity shall implement, in a manner that identifies, assesses, and corrects deficiencies, a cyber security training program(s) appropriate to individual roles, functions, or responsibilities that collectively includes each of the applicable requirement parts in CIP-004-5.1 Table R2 – Cyber Security Training Program.	

Mapping of NIST Cybersecurity Framework v1.0 to NERC CIP version 5 & C2M2 Practices

Function	Category	Subcategory	C2M2 Practices **			NERC CIP v5
			MIL 1	MIL 2	MIL 3	
PROTECT (PR)	**Awareness and Training (AT):** The organization's personnel and partners are provided cybersecurity awareness education and are adequately trained to perform their information security-related duties and responsibilities consistent with related policies, procedures, and agreements.	**PR.AT-5:** Physical and information security personnel understand roles & responsibilities	WM-1a WM-1b	WM-1c WM-1d	WM-1e WM-1f WM-1g	CIP-006-5 R2: Each Responsible Entity shall implement, in a manner that identifies, assesses, and corrects deficiencies, one or more documented visitor control programs that include each of the applicable requirement parts in CIP-005-5 Table R2 - Visitor Control Program)
PROTECT (PR)	**Data Security (DS):** Information and records (data) are managed consistent with the organization's risk strategy to protect the confidentiality, integrity, and availability of information.	**PR.DS-1:** Data-at-rest is protected	ACM-1b TVM-1c TVM-2c	CPM-3b	ACM-1e TVM-2i TVM-2n	CIP-003-5 R1 - 1.8: Each Responsible Entity, for its high impact and medium impact BES Cyber Systems, shall review and obtain CIP Senior Manager approval at least once every 15 calendar months for one or more documented cyber security policies that collectively address the following topics: Information protection (CIP-011);
PROTECT (PR)	**Data Security (DS):** Information and records (data) are managed consistent with the organization's risk strategy to protect the confidentiality, integrity, and availability of information.	**PR.DS-1:** Data-at-rest is protected	ACM-1b TVM-1c TVM-2c	CPM-3b	ACM-1e TVM-2i TVM-2n	CIP-004-5.1 R4: Each Responsible Entity shall implement, in a manner that identifies, assesses, and corrects deficiencies, one or more documented access management programs that collectively include each of the applicable requirement parts in CIP-004-5.1 Table R4 – Access Management Program.
PROTECT (PR)	**Data Security (DS):** Information and records (data) are managed consistent with the organization's risk strategy to protect the confidentiality, integrity, and availability of information.	**PR.DS-1:** Data-at-rest is protected	ACM-1b TVM-1c TVM-2c	CPM-3b	ACM-1e TVM-2i TVM-2n	CIP-004-5.1 R5: Each Responsible Entity shall implement, in a manner that identifies, assesses, and corrects deficiencies, one or more documented access revocation programs that collectively include each of the applicable requirement parts in CIP-004-5.1 Table R5 – Access Revocation.

Mapping of NIST Cybersecurity Framework v1.0 to NERC CIP version 5 & C2M2 Practices

Function	Category	Subcategory	C2M2 Practices **			NERC CIP v5
			MIL 1	MIL 2	MIL 3	
PROTECT (PR)	**Data Security (DS):** Information and records (data) are managed consistent with the organization's risk strategy to protect the confidentiality, integrity, and availability of information.	**PR.DS-1:** Data-at-rest is protected	ACM-1b TVM-1c TVM-2c	CPM-3b	ACM-1e TVM-2i TVM-2n	CIP-007-5 R3: Each Responsible Entity shall implement, in a manner that identifies, assesses, and corrects deficiencies, one or more documented processes that collectively include each of the applicable requirement parts in CIP-007-5 Table R3 – Malicious Code Prevention.
PROTECT (PR)	**Data Security (DS):** Information and records (data) are managed consistent with the organization's risk strategy to protect the confidentiality, integrity, and availability of information.	**PR.DS-1:** Data-at-rest is protected	ACM-1b TVM-1c TVM-2c	CPM-3b	ACM-1e TVM-2i TVM-2n	CIP-011-1 R1: Each Responsible Entity shall implement, in a Manner that identifies, assesses, and corrects deficiencies, one or more documented information protection program(s) that collectively includes each of the applicable requirement parts in CIP-011-1 Table R1 – Information Protection.
PROTECT (PR)	**Data Security (DS):** Information and records (data) are managed consistent with the organization's risk strategy to protect the confidentiality, integrity, and availability of information.	**PR.DS-1:** Data-at-rest is protected	ACM-1b TVM-1c TVM-2c	CPM-3b	ACM-1e TVM-2i TVM-2n	CIP-011-1 R2: Each Responsible Entity shall implement one or more documented processes that collectively include the applicable requirement parts in CIP-011-1 Table R2 – BES Cyber Asset Reuse and Disposal.
PROTECT (PR)	**Data Security (DS):** Information and records (data) are managed consistent with the organization's risk strategy to protect the confidentiality, integrity, and availability of information.	**PR.DS-2:** Data-in-transit is protected	ACM-1b TVM-1c TVM-2c	CPM-3b	ACM-1e TVM-2i TVM-2n	CIP-003-5 R1 - 1.2: Each Responsible Entity, for its high impact and medium impact BES Cyber Systems, shall review and obtain CIP Senior Manager approval at least once every 15 calendar months for one or more documented cyber security policies that collectively address the following topics: Electronic Security Perimeters (CIP-005) including Interactive Remote Access;

80

Mapping of NIST Cybersecurity Framework v1.0 to NERC CIP version 5 & C2M2 Practices

Function	Category	Subcategory	C2M2 Practices **			NERC CIP v5
			MIL 1	MIL 2	MIL 3	
PROTECT (PR)	**Data Security (DS):** Information and records (data) are managed consistent with the organization's risk strategy to protect the confidentiality, integrity, and availability of information.	**PR.DS-2:** Data-in-transit is protected	ACM-1b TVM-1c TVM-2c	CPM-3b	ACM-1e TVM-2i TVM-2n	CIP-003-5 R1 – 1.8: Each Responsible Entity, for its high impact and medium impact BES Cyber Systems, shall review and obtain CIP Senior Manager approval at least once every 15 calendar months for one or more documented cyber security policies that collectively address the following topics: Information protection (CIP-011);
PROTECT (PR)	**Data Security (DS):** Information and records (data) are managed consistent with the organization's risk strategy to protect the confidentiality, integrity, and availability of information.	**PR.DS-2:** Data-in-transit is protected	ACM-1b TVM-1c TVM-2c	CPM-3b	ACM-1e TVM-2i TVM-2n	CIP-003-5 R2 – 2.3: Each Responsible Entity for its assets identified in CIP-002-5, Requirement R1, Part R1.3 (i.e., low impact), shall implement, in a manner that identifies, assesses, and corrects deficiencies, one or more documented cyber security policies that collectively address the following topics, and review and obtain CIP Senior Manager approval for those policies at least once every 15 calendar months: Electronic access controls for external routable protocol connections and Dial-up Connectivity
PROTECT (PR)	**Data Security (DS):** Information and records (data) are managed consistent with the organization's risk strategy to protect the confidentiality, integrity, and availability of information.	**PR.DS-2:** Data-in-transit is protected	ACM-1b TVM-1c TVM-2c	CPM-3b	ACM-1e TVM-2i TVM-2n	CIP-004-5.1 R4: Each Responsible Entity shall implement, in a manner that identifies, assesses, and corrects deficiencies, one or more documented access management programs that collectively include each of the applicable requirement parts in CIP-004-5.1 Table R4 – Access Management Program.
PROTECT (PR)	**Data Security (DS):** Information and records (data) are managed consistent with the organization's risk strategy to protect the confidentiality, integrity, and availability of information.	**PR.DS-2:** Data-in-transit is protected	ACM-1b TVM-1c TVM-2c	CPM-3b	ACM-1e TVM-2i TVM-2n	CIP-004-5.1 R5: Each Responsible Entity shall implement, in a manner that identifies, assesses, and corrects deficiencies, one or more documented access revocation programs that collectively include each of the applicable

Mapping of NIST Cybersecurity Framework v1.0 to NERC CIP version 5 & C2M2 Practices						
Function	Category	Subcategory	C2M2 Practices **			NERC CIP v5
			MIL 1	MIL 2	MIL 3	
						requirement parts in CIP-004-5.1 Table R5 – Access Revocation.
PROTECT (PR)	Data Security (DS): Information and records (data) are managed consistent with the organization's risk strategy to protect the confidentiality, integrity, and availability of information.	PR.DS-2: Data-in-transit is protected	ACM-1b TVM-1c TVM-2c	CPM-3b	ACM-1e TVM-2i TVM-2n	CIP-005-5 R1: Each Responsible Entity shall implement one or more documented processes that collectively include each of the applicable requirement parts in CIP-005-5 Table R1 – Electronic Security Perimeter.
PROTECT (PR)	Data Security (DS): Information and records (data) are managed consistent with the organization's risk strategy to protect the confidentiality, integrity, and availability of information.	PR.DS-2: Data-in-transit is protected	ACM-1b TVM-1c TVM-2c	CPM-3b	ACM-1e TVM-2i TVM-2n	CIP-005-5 R2: Each Responsible Entity allowing Interactive Remote Access to BES Cyber Systems shall implement one or more documented processes that collectively include the applicable requirement parts, where technically feasible, in CIP-005-5 Table R2 – Interactive Remote Access Management.
PROTECT (PR)	Data Security (DS): Information and records (data) are managed consistent with the organization's risk strategy to protect the confidentiality, integrity, and availability of information.	PR.DS-2: Data-in-transit is protected	ACM-1b TVM-1c TVM-2c	CPM-3b	ACM-1e TVM-2i TVM-2n	CIP-007-5 R3: Each Responsible Entity shall implement, in a manner that identifies, assesses, and corrects deficiencies, one or more documented processes that collectively include each of the applicable requirement parts in CIP-007-5 Table R3 – Malicious Code Prevention.
PROTECT (PR)	Data Security (DS): Information and records (data) are managed consistent with the organization's risk strategy to protect the confidentiality, integrity, and availability of information.	PR.DS-2: Data-in-transit is protected	ACM-1b TVM-1c TVM-2c	CPM-3b	ACM-1e TVM-2i TVM-2n	CIP-011-1 R1: Each Responsible Entity shall implement, in a Manner that identifies, assesses, and corrects deficiencies, one or more documented information protection program(s) that collectively includes each of the applicable requirement parts in CIP-011-1 Table R1 – Information Protection.

Mapping of NIST Cybersecurity Framework v1.0 to NERC CIP version 5 & C2M2 Practices

Function	Category	Subcategory	C2M2 Practices **			NERC CIP v5
			MIL 1	MIL 2	MIL 3	
PROTECT (PR)	**Data Security (DS):** Information and records (data) are managed consistent with the organization's risk strategy to protect the confidentiality, integrity, and availability of information.	**PR.DS-3:** Assets are formally managed throughout removal, transfers, and disposition	ACM-1a ACM-1b ACM-2a ACM-2b ACM-3a ACM-3b	ACM-1c ACM-1d ACM-2c ACM-3c ACM-3d ACM-4a ACM-4b ACM-4c ACM-4d	ACM-1e ACM-1f ACM-2d ACM-2e ACM-3e ACM-3f ACM-4e ACM-4f ACM-4g ACM-4h ACM-4i	CIP-011-1 R2: Each Responsible Entity shall implement one or more documented processes that collectively include the applicable requirement parts in CIP-011-1 Table R2 – BES Cyber Asset Reuse and Disposal.
PROTECT (PR)	**Data Security (DS):** Information and records (data) are managed consistent with the organization's risk strategy to protect the confidentiality, integrity, and availability of information.	**PR.DS-4:** Adequate capacity to ensure availability is maintained	TVM-1c TVM-2c	CPM-3b	TVM-2i TVM-2n	CIP-003-5 R1 - 1.6: Each Responsible Entity, for its high impact and medium impact BES Cyber Systems, shall review and obtain CIP Senior Manager approval at least once every 15 calendar months for one or more documented cyber security policies that collectively address the following topics: Recovery plans for BES Cyber Systems (CIP-009);
PROTECT (PR)	**Data Security (DS):** Information and records (data) are managed consistent with the organization's risk strategy to protect the confidentiality, integrity, and availability of information.	**PR.DS-4:** Adequate capacity to ensure availability is maintained	TVM-1c TVM-2c	CPM-3b	TVM-2i TVM-2n	CIP-007-5 R4 - 4.3: Where technically feasible, retain applicable event logs identified in Part 4.1 for at least the last 90 consecutive calendar days except under CIP Exceptional Circumstances.

Mapping of NIST Cybersecurity Framework v1.0 to NERC CIP version 5 & C2M2 Practices

Function	Category	Subcategory	C2M2 Practices **			NERC CIP v5
			MIL 1	MIL 2	MIL 3	
PROTECT (PR)	Data Security (DS): Information and records (data) are managed consistent with the organization's risk strategy to protect the confidentiality, integrity, and availability of information.	PR.DS-4: Adequate capacity to ensure availability is maintained	TVM-1c TVM-2c	CPM-3b	TVM-2i TVM-2n	CIP-009-5 R1: Each Responsible Entity shall have one or more documented recovery plans that collectively include each of the applicable requirement parts in CIP-009-5 Table R1 – Recovery Plan Specifications.
PROTECT (PR)	Data Security (DS): Information and records (data) are managed consistent with the organization's risk strategy to protect the confidentiality, integrity, and availability of information.	PR.DS-4: Adequate capacity to ensure availability is maintained	TVM-1c TVM-2c	CPM-3b	TVM-2i TVM-2n	CIP-007-5 R3: Each Responsible Entity shall implement, in a manner that identifies, assesses, and corrects deficiencies, one or more documented processes that collectively include each of the applicable requirement parts in CIP-007-5 Table R3 – Malicious Code Prevention.
PROTECT (PR)	Data Security (DS): Information and records (data) are managed consistent with the organization's risk strategy to protect the confidentiality, integrity, and availability of information.	PR.DS-5: Protections against data leaks are implemented	TVM-1c TVM-2c	CPM-3b	TVM-2i TVM-2n	CIP-003-5 R1 - 1.2: Each Responsible Entity, for its high impact and medium impact BES Cyber Systems, shall review and obtain CIP Senior Manager approval at least once every 15 calendar months for one or more documented cyber security policies that collectively address the following topics: Electronic Security Perimeters (CIP-005) including Interactive Remote Access;
PROTECT (PR)	Data Security (DS): Information and records (data) are managed consistent with the organization's risk strategy to protect the confidentiality, integrity, and availability of information.	PR.DS-5: Protections against data leaks are implemented	TVM-1c TVM-2c	CPM-3b	TVM-2i TVM-2n	CIP-003-5 R1 - 1.4: Each Responsible Entity, for its high impact and medium impact BES Cyber Systems, shall review and obtain CIP Senior Manager approval at least once every 15 calendar months for one or more documented cyber security policies that collectively address the following topics: System security management (CIP-007);

Mapping of NIST Cybersecurity Framework v1.0 to NERC CIP version 5 & C2M2 Practices

Function	Category	Subcategory	C2M2 Practices **			NERC CIP v5
			MIL 1	MIL 2	MIL 3	
PROTECT (PR)	**Data Security (DS):** Information and records (data) are managed consistent with the organization's risk strategy to protect the confidentiality, integrity, and availability of information.	**PR.DS-5:** Protections against data leaks are implemented	TVM-1c TVM-2c	CPM-3b	TVM-2i TVM-2n	CIP-003-5 R1 – 1.8: Each Responsible Entity, for its high impact and medium impact BES Cyber Systems, shall review and obtain CIP Senior Manager approval at least once every 15 calendar months for one or more documented cyber security policies that collectively address the following topics: Information protection (CIP-011);
PROTECT (PR)	**Data Security (DS):** Information and records (data) are managed consistent with the organization's risk strategy to protect the confidentiality, integrity, and availability of information.	**PR.DS-5:** Protections against data leaks are implemented	TVM-1c TVM-2c	CPM-3b	TVM-2i TVM-2n	CIP-003-5 R2 – 2.3: Each Responsible Entity for its assets identified in CIP-002-5, Requirement R1, Part R1.3 (ie: low impact), shall implement, in a manner that identifies, assesses, and corrects deficiencies, one or more documented cyber security policies that collectively address the following topics, and review and obtain CIP Senior Manager approval for those policies at least once every 15 calendar months: Electronic access controls for external routable protocol connections and Dial-up Connectivity
PROTECT (PR)	**Data Security (DS):** Information and records (data) are managed consistent with the organization's risk strategy to protect the confidentiality, integrity, and availability of information.	**PR.DS-5:** Protections against data leaks are implemented	TVM-1c TVM-2c	CPM-3b	TVM-2i TVM-2n	CIP-004-5.1 R4: Each Responsible Entity shall implement, in a manner that identifies, assesses, and corrects deficiencies, one or more documented access management programs that collectively include each of the applicable requirement parts in CIP-004-5.1 Table R4 – Access Management Program.
PROTECT (PR)	**Data Security (DS):** Information and records (data) are managed consistent with the organization's risk strategy to protect the confidentiality, integrity, and availability of information.	**PR.DS-5:** Protections against data leaks are implemented	TVM-1c TVM-2c	CPM-3b	TVM-2i TVM-2n	CIP-004-5.1 R5: Each Responsible Entity shall implement, in a manner that identifies, assesses, and corrects deficiencies, one or more documented access revocation programs that collectively include each of the applicable

Mapping of NIST Cybersecurity Framework v1.0 to NERC CIP version 5 & C2M2 Practices

Function	Category	Subcategory	C2M2 Practices **			NERC CIP v5
			MIL 1	MIL 2	MIL 3	
						requirement parts in CIP-004-5.1 Table R5 – Access Revocation.
PROTECT (PR)	**Data Security (DS)**: Information and records (data) are managed consistent with the organization's risk strategy to protect the confidentiality, integrity, and availability of information.	**PR.DS-5**: Protections against data leaks are implemented	TVM-1c TVM-2c	CPM-3b	TVM-2i TVM-2n	CIP-005-5 R1: Each Responsible Entity shall implement one or more documented processes that collectively include each of the applicable requirement parts in CIP-005-5 Table R1 – Electronic Security Perimeter.
PROTECT (PR)	**Data Security (DS)**: Information and records (data) are managed consistent with the organization's risk strategy to protect the confidentiality, integrity, and availability of information.	**PR.DS-5**: Protections against data leaks are implemented	TVM-1c TVM-2c	CPM-3b	TVM-2i TVM-2n	CIP-005-5 R2: Each Responsible Entity allowing Interactive Remote Access to BES Cyber Systems shall implement one or more documented processes that collectively include the applicable requirement parts, where technically feasible, in CIP-005-5 Table R2 – Interactive Remote Access Management.
PROTECT (PR)	**Data Security (DS)**: Information and records (data) are managed consistent with the organization's risk strategy to protect the confidentiality, integrity, and availability of information.	**PR.DS-5**: Protections against data leaks are implemented	TVM-1c TVM-2c	CPM-3b	TVM-2i TVM-2n	CIP-007-5 R3: Each Responsible Entity shall implement, in a manner that identifies, assesses, and corrects deficiencies, one or more documented processes that collectively include each of the applicable requirement parts in CIP-007-5 Table R3 – Malicious Code Prevention.
PROTECT (PR)	**Data Security (DS)**: Information and records (data) are managed consistent with the organization's risk strategy to protect the confidentiality, integrity, and availability of information.	**PR.DS-5**: Protections against data leaks are implemented	TVM-1c TVM-2c	CPM-3b	TVM-2i TVM-2n	CIP-007-5 R4: Each Responsible Entity shall implement, in a manner that identifies, assesses, and corrects deficiencies, one or more documented processes that collectively include each of the applicable requirement parts in CIP-007-5 Table R4 – Security Event Monitoring.

Mapping of NIST Cybersecurity Framework v1.0 to NERC CIP version 5 & C2M2 Practices

Function	Category	Subcategory	C2M2 Practices **			NERC CIP v5
			MIL 1	MIL 2	MIL 3	
PROTECT (PR)	**Data Security (DS):** Information and records (data) are managed consistent with the organization's risk strategy to protect the confidentiality, integrity, and availability of information.	**PR.DS-5:** Protections against data leaks are implemented	TVM-1c TVM-2c	CPM-3b	TVM-2i TVM-2n	CIP-007-5 R5: Each Responsible Entity shall implement, in a manner that identifies, assesses, and corrects deficiencies, one or more documented processes that collectively include each of the applicable requirement parts in CIP-007-5 Table R5 – System Access Controls.
PROTECT (PR)	**Data Security (DS):** Information and records (data) are managed consistent with the organization's risk strategy to protect the confidentiality, integrity, and availability of information.	**PR.DS-5:** Protections against data leaks are implemented	TVM-1c TVM-2c	CPM-3b	TVM-2i TVM-2n	CIP-011-1 R1: Each Responsible Entity shall implement, in a Manner that identifies, assesses, and corrects deficiencies, one or more documented information protection program(s) that collectively includes each of the applicable requirement parts in CIP-011-1 Table R1 – Information Protection.
PROTECT (PR)	**Data Security (DS):** Information and records (data) are managed consistent with the organization's risk strategy to protect the confidentiality, integrity, and availability of information.	**PR.DS-5:** Protections against data leaks are implemented	TVM-1c TVM-2c	CPM-3b	TVM-2i TVM-2n	CIP-011-1 R2: Each Responsible Entity shall implement one or more documented processes that collectively include the applicable requirement parts in CIP-011-1 Table R2 – BES Cyber Asset Reuse and Disposal.
PROTECT (PR)	**Data Security (DS):** Information and records (data) are managed consistent with the organization's risk strategy to protect the confidentiality, integrity, and availability of information.	**PR.DS-6:** Integrity checking mechanisms are used to verify software, firmware, and information integrity		ACM-3d		CIP-003-5 R1 - 1.7: Each Responsible Entity, for its high impact and medium impact BES Cyber Systems, shall review and obtain CIP Senior Manager approval at least once every 15 calendar months for one or more documented cyber security policies that collectively address the following topics: Configuration change management and vulnerability assessments (CIP-010);

Mapping of NIST Cybersecurity Framework v1.0 to NERC CIP version 5 & C2M2 Practices

Function	Category	Subcategory	C2M2 Practices **			NERC CIP v5
			MIL 1	MIL 2	MIL 3	
PROTECT (PR)	Data Security (DS): Information and records (data) are managed consistent with the organization's risk strategy to protect the confidentiality, integrity, and availability of information.	PR.DS-6: Integrity checking mechanisms are used to verify software, firmware, and information integrity		ACM-3d		CIP-010-1 R1: Each Responsible Entity shall implement, in a manner that identifies, assesses, and corrects deficiencies, one or more documented processes that collectively include each of the applicable requirement parts in CIP-010-1 Table R1 – Configuration Change Management.
PROTECT (PR)	Data Security (DS): Information and records (data) are managed consistent with the organization's risk strategy to protect the confidentiality, integrity, and availability of information.	PR.DS-6: Integrity checking mechanisms are used to verify software, firmware, and information integrity		ACM-3d		CIP-010-1 R2: Each Responsible Entity shall implement, in a manner that identifies, assesses, and corrects deficiencies, one or more documented processes that collectively include each of the applicable requirement parts in CIP-010-1 Table R2 – Configuration Monitoring.
PROTECT (PR)	Data Security (DS): Information and records (data) are managed consistent with the organization's risk strategy to protect the confidentiality, integrity, and availability of information.	PR.DS-7: The development and testing environment(s) are separate from the production environment		ACM-3c	ACM-3e	CIP-003-5 R1 - 1.2: Each Responsible Entity, for its high impact and medium impact BES Cyber Systems, shall review and obtain CIP Senior Manager approval at least once every 15 calendar months for one or more documented cyber security policies that collectively address the following topics: Electronic Security Perimeters (CIP-005) including Interactive Remote Access;
PROTECT (PR)	Data Security (DS): Information and records (data) are managed consistent with the organization's risk strategy to protect the confidentiality, integrity, and availability of information.	PR.DS-7: The development and testing environment(s) are separate from the production environment		ACM-3c	ACM-3e	CIP-003-5 R1 - 1.7: Each Responsible Entity, for its high impact and medium impact BES Cyber Systems, shall review and obtain CIP Senior Manager approval at least once every 15 calendar months for one or more documented cyber security policies that collectively address the following topics: Configuration change management and vulnerability assessments (CIP-010);

Mapping of NIST Cybersecurity Framework v1.0 to NERC CIP version 5 & C2M2 Practices

Function	Category	Subcategory	C2M2 Practices **			NERC CIP v5
			MIL 1	MIL 2	MIL 3	
PROTECT (PR)	**Data Security (DS):** Information and records (data) are managed consistent with the organization's risk strategy to protect the confidentiality, integrity, and availability of information.	**PR.DS-7:** The development and testing environment(s) are separate from the production environment		ACM-3c	ACM-3e	CIP-005-5 R1: Each Responsible Entity shall implement one or more documented processes that collectively include each of the applicable requirement parts in CIP-005-5 Table R1 – Electronic Security Perimeter.
PROTECT (PR)	**Data Security (DS):** Information and records (data) are managed consistent with the organization's risk strategy to protect the confidentiality, integrity, and availability of information.	**PR.DS-7:** The development and testing environment(s) are separate from the production environment		ACM-3c	ACM-3e	CIP-010-1 R2: Each Responsible Entity shall implement, in a manner that identifies, assesses, and corrects deficiencies, one or more documented processes that collectively include each of the applicable requirement parts in CIP-010-1 Table R2 – Configuration Monitoring.
PROTECT (PR)	**Information Protection Processes and Procedures (IP):** Security policies (that address purpose, scope, roles, responsibilities, management commitment, and coordination among organizational entities), processes, and procedures are maintained and used to manage protection of information systems and assets.	**PR.IP-1:** A baseline configuration of information technology/industrial control systems is created and maintained	ACM-2a ACM-2b	ACM-2c	ACM-2d ACM-2e	CIP-010-1 R1: Each Responsible Entity shall implement, in a manner that identifies, assesses, and corrects deficiencies, one or more documented processes that collectively include each of the applicable requirement parts in CIP-010-1 Table R1 – Configuration Change Management.
PROTECT (PR)	**Information Protection Processes and Procedures (IP):** Security policies (that address purpose, scope, roles, responsibilities, management commitment, and coordination among organizational entities), processes, and procedures are maintained and used to manage protection of information systems and assets.	**PR.IP-1:** A baseline configuration of information technology/industrial control systems is created and maintained	ACM-2a ACM-2b	ACM-2c	ACM-2d ACM-2e	CIP-010-1 R2: Each Responsible Entity shall implement, in a manner that identifies, assesses, and corrects deficiencies, one or more documented processes that collectively include each of the applicable requirement parts in CIP-010-1 Table R2 – Configuration Monitoring.

Mapping of NIST Cybersecurity Framework v1.0 to NERC CIP version 5 & C2M2 Practices

Function	Category	Subcategory	C2M2 Practices **			NERC CIP v5
			MIL 1	MIL 2	MIL 3	
PROTECT (PR)	**Information Protection Processes and Procedures (IP):** Security policies (that address purpose, scope, roles, responsibilities, management commitment, and coordination among organizational entities), processes, and procedures are maintained and used to manage protection of information systems and assets.	**PR.IP-2:** A System Development Life Cycle to manage systems is implemented		ACM-3d		
PROTECT (PR)	**Information Protection Processes and Procedures (IP):** Security policies (that address purpose, scope, roles, responsibilities, management commitment, and coordination among organizational entities), processes, and procedures are maintained and used to manage protection of information systems and assets.	**PR.IP-3:** Configuration change control processes are in place	ACM-3a ACM-3b	ACM-3c ACM-3d	ACM-3e ACM-3f	CIP-003-5 R1 - 1.4: Each Responsible Entity, for its high impact and medium impact BES Cyber Systems, shall review and obtain CIP Senior Manager approval at least once every 15 calendar months for one or more documented cyber security policies that collectively address the following topics: System security management (CIP-007);
PROTECT (PR)	**Information Protection Processes and Procedures (IP):** Security policies (that address purpose, scope, roles, responsibilities, management commitment, and coordination among organizational entities), processes, and procedures are maintained and used to manage protection of information systems and assets.	**PR.IP-3:** Configuration change control processes are in place	ACM-3a ACM-3b	ACM-3c ACM-3d	ACM-3e ACM-3f	CIP-003-5 R1 - 1.7: Each Responsible Entity, for its high impact and medium impact BES Cyber Systems, shall review and obtain CIP Senior Manager approval at least once every 15 calendar months for one or more documented cyber security policies that collectively address the following topics: Configuration change management and vulnerability assessments (CIP-010);

90

Mapping of NIST Cybersecurity Framework v1.0 to NERC CIP version 5 & C2M2 Practices

Function	Category	Subcategory	C2M2 Practices **			NERC CIP v5
			MIL 1	MIL 2	MIL 3	
PROTECT (PR)	**Information Protection Processes and Procedures (IP):** Security policies (that address purpose, scope, roles, responsibilities, management commitment, and coordination among organizational entities), processes, and procedures are maintained and used to manage protection of information systems and assets.	**PR.IP-3:** Configuration change control processes are in place	ACM-3a ACM-3b	ACM-3c ACM-3d	ACM-3e ACM-3f	CIP-010-1 R1: Each Responsible Entity shall implement, in a manner that identifies, assesses, and corrects deficiencies, one or more documented processes that collectively include each of the applicable requirement parts in CIP-010-1 Table R1 – Configuration Change Management.
PROTECT (PR)	**Information Protection Processes and Procedures (IP):** Security policies (that address purpose, scope, roles, responsibilities, management commitment, and coordination among organizational entities), processes, and procedures are maintained and used to manage protection of information systems and assets.	**PR.IP-3:** Configuration change control processes are in place	ACM-3a ACM-3b	ACM-3c ACM-3d	ACM-3e ACM-3f	CIP-010-1 R2: Each Responsible Entity shall implement, in a manner that identifies, assesses, and corrects deficiencies, one or more documented processes that collectively include each of the applicable requirement parts in CIP-010-1 Table R2 – Configuration Monitoring.
PROTECT (PR)	**Information Protection Processes and Procedures (IP):** Security policies (that address purpose, scope, roles, responsibilities, management commitment, and coordination among organizational entities), processes, and procedures are maintained and used to manage protection of information systems and assets.	**PR.IP-4:** Backups of information are conducted, maintained, and tested periodically	IR-4a IR-4b IR-4c	IR-4f	IR-4g IR-4j	CIP-009-5 R1: Each Responsible Entity shall have one or more documented recovery plans that collectively include each of the applicable requirement parts in CIP-009-5 Table R1 - Recovery Plan Specifications.

Mapping of NIST Cybersecurity Framework v1.0 to NERC CIP version 5 & C2M2 Practices

Function	Category	Subcategory	C2M2 Practices **			NERC CIP v5
			MIL 1	MIL 2	MIL 3	
PROTECT (PR)	**Information Protection Processes and Procedures (IP):** Security policies (that address purpose, scope, roles, responsibilities, management commitment, and coordination among organizational entities), processes, and procedures are maintained and used to manage protection of information systems and assets.	**PR.IP-4:** Backups of information are conducted, maintained, and tested periodically	IR-4a IR-4b IR-4c	IR-4f	IR-4g IR-4j	CIP-009-5 R3: Each Responsible Entity shall maintain each of its recovery plans in accordance with each of the applicable requirement parts in CIP-009-5 Table R3 – Recovery Plan Review, Update and Communication.
PROTECT (PR)	**Information Protection Processes and Procedures (IP):** Security policies (that address purpose, scope, roles, responsibilities, management commitment, and coordination among organizational entities), processes, and procedures are maintained and used to manage protection of information systems and assets.	**PR.IP-5:** Policy and regulations regarding the physical operating environment for organizational assets are met	RM-2b IAM-2a		RM-3f IAM-3f	CIP-003-5 R1 - 1.1 to 1.9: Each Responsible Entity, for its high impact and medium impact BES Cyber Systems, shall review and obtain CIP Senior Manager approval at least once every 15 calendar months for one or more documented cyber security policies that collectively address the following topics: 1.1 Personnel & training (CIP-004) 1.2 Electronic Security Perimeters (CIP005) including interactive Remote Access, 1.3 Physical Security of BES Cyber Systems (CIP006), 1.4 System security management (CIP007), 1.5 Incident reporting and response planning (CIP008), 1.6 Recovery plans for BES Cyber Systems (CIP009), 1.7 Configuration change management and vulnerability assessments (CIP010), 1.8 Information protection (CIP011) and 1.9 Declaring and responding to CIP Exceptional Circumstances.

Mapping of NIST Cybersecurity Framework v1.0 to NERC CIP version 5 & C2M2 Practices

Function	Category	Subcategory	C2M2 Practices **			NERC CIP v5
			MIL 1	MIL 2	MIL 3	
PROTECT (PR)	**Information Protection Processes and Procedures (IP):** Security policies (that address purpose, scope, roles, responsibilities, management commitment, and coordination among organizational entities), processes, and procedures are maintained and used to manage protection of information systems and assets.	**PR.IP-6:** Data is destroyed according to policy		ACM-3d		CIP-011-1 R2: Each Responsible Entity shall implement one or more documented processes that collectively include the applicable requirement parts in CIP-011-1 Table R2 – BES Cyber Asset Reuse and Disposal.
PROTECT (PR)	**Information Protection Processes and Procedures (IP):** Security policies (that address purpose, scope, roles, responsibilities, management commitment, and coordination among organizational entities), processes, and procedures are maintained and used to manage protection of information systems and assets.	**PR.IP-7:** Protection processes are continuously improved		TVM-1h	CPM-1g	CIP-010-1 R3: Each Responsible Entity shall implement one or more documented processes that collectively include each of the applicable requirement parts in CIP-010-1 Table R3– Vulnerability Assessments.
PROTECT (PR)	**Information Protection Processes and Procedures (IP):** Security policies (that address purpose, scope, roles, responsibilities, management commitment, and coordination among organizational entities), processes, and procedures are maintained and used to manage protection of information systems and assets.	**PR.IP-8:** Effectiveness of protection technologies is shared with appropriate parties	ISC-1a ISC-1b	ISC-1c ISC-1d ISC-1e ISC-1f ISC-1g ISC-2b	ISC-1h ISC-1i ISC-1j ISC-1k ISC-1l	CIP-008-5 R3: Each Responsible Entity shall maintain each of its Cyber Security Incident response plans according to each of the applicable requirement parts in CIP-008-5 Table R3 – Cyber Security Incident Response Plan Review, Update, and Communication.

Mapping of NIST Cybersecurity Framework v1.0 to NERC CIP version 5 & C2M2 Practices

Function	Category	Subcategory	C2M2 Practices **			NERC CIP v5
			MIL 1	MIL 2	MIL 3	
PROTECT (PR)	**Information Protection Processes and Procedures (IP):** Security policies (that address purpose, scope, roles, responsibilities, management commitment, and coordination among organizational entities), processes, and procedures are maintained and used to manage protection of information systems and assets.	**PR.IP-8:** Effectiveness of protection technologies is shared with appropriate parties	ISC-1a ISC-1b	ISC-1c ISC-1d ISC-1e ISC-1f ISC-1g ISC-2b	ISC-1h ISC-1i ISC-1j ISC-1k ISC-1l	CIP-010-1 R3: Each Responsible Entity shall implement one or more documented processes that collectively include each of the applicable requirement parts in CIP-010-1 Table R3– Vulnerability Assessments.
PROTECT (PR)	**Information Protection Processes and Procedures (IP):** Security policies (that address purpose, scope, roles, responsibilities, management commitment, and coordination among organizational entities), processes, and procedures are maintained and used to manage protection of information systems and assets.	**PR.IP-9:** Response plans (Incident Response and Business Continuity) and recovery plans (Incident Recovery and Disaster Recovery) are in place and managed	IR-4c	IR-3e IR-3f IR-4d IR-4f IR-5a IR-5b IR-5c IR-5d RM-1a RM-1b TVM-1d	IR-3k IR-3m IR-4i IR-4j IR-5e IR-5f IR-5g IR-5h IR-5i RM-1c	CIP-003-5 R1 - 1.5: Each Responsible Entity, for its high impact and medium impact BES Cyber Systems, shall review and obtain CIP Senior Manager approval at least once every 15 calendar months for one or more documented cyber security policies that collectively address the following topics: Incident reporting and response planning (CIP-008);
PROTECT (PR)	**Information Protection Processes and Procedures (IP):** Security policies (that address purpose, scope, roles, responsibilities, management commitment, and coordination among organizational entities), processes, and procedures are maintained and used to manage protection of information systems and assets.	**PR.IP-9:** Response plans (Incident Response and Business Continuity) and recovery plans (Incident Recovery and Disaster Recovery) are in place and managed	IR-4c	IR-3e IR-3f IR-4d IR-4f IR-5a IR-5b IR-5c IR-5d RM-1a RM-1b TVM-1d	IR-3k IR-3m IR-4i IR-4j IR-5e IR-5f IR-5g IR-5h IR-5i RM-1c	CIP-003-5 R1 - 1.6: Each Responsible Entity, for its high impact and medium impact BES Cyber Systems, shall review and obtain CIP Senior Manager approval at least once every 15 calendar months for one or more documented cyber security policies that collectively address the following topics: Recovery plans for BES Cyber Systems (CIP-009);

Mapping of NIST Cybersecurity Framework v1.0 to NERC CIP version 5 & C2M2 Practices

Function	Category	Subcategory	C2M2 Practices **			NERC CIP v5
			MIL 1	MIL 2	MIL 3	
PROTECT (PR)	**Information Protection Processes and Procedures (IP):** Security policies (that address purpose, scope, roles, responsibilities, management commitment, and coordination among organizational entities), processes, and procedures are maintained and used to manage protection of information systems and assets.	**PR.IP-9:** Response plans (Incident Response and Business Continuity) and recovery plans (Incident Recovery and Disaster Recovery) are in place and managed	IR-4c	IR-3e IR-3f IR-4d IR-4f IR-5a IR-5b IR-5c IR-5d RM-1a RM-1b TVM-1d	IR-3k IR-3m IR-4i IR-4j IR-5e IR-5f IR-5g IR-5h IR-5i RM-1c	CIP-003-5 R2 - 2.4: Each Responsible Entity for its assets identified in CIP-002-5, Requirement R1, Part R1.3, shall implement, in a manner that identifies, assesses, and corrects deficiencies, one or more documented cyber security policies that collectively address the following topics, and review and obtain CIP Senior Manager approval for those policies at least once every 15 calendar months: (An inventory, list, or discrete identification of low impact BES Cyber Systems or their BES Cyber Assets is not required). Incident response to a Cyber Security Incident.
PROTECT (PR)	**Information Protection Processes and Procedures (IP):** Security policies (that address purpose, scope, roles, responsibilities, management commitment, and coordination among organizational entities), processes, and procedures are maintained and used to manage protection of information systems and assets.	**PR.IP-9:** Response plans (Incident Response and Business Continuity) and recovery plans (Incident Recovery and Disaster Recovery) are in place and managed	IR-4c	IR-3e IR-3f IR-4d IR-4f IR-5a IR-5b IR-5c IR-5d RM-1a RM-1b TVM-1d	IR-3k IR-3m IR-4i IR-4j IR-5e IR-5f IR-5g IR-5h IR-5i RM-1c	CIP-008-5 R1: Each Responsible Entity shall document one or more Cyber Security Incident response plan(s) that collectively include each of the applicable requirement parts in CIP-008-5 Table R1 – Cyber Security Incident Response Plan Specifications.

Mapping of NIST Cybersecurity Framework v1.0 to NERC CIP version 5 & C2M2 Practices					
			C2M2 Practices **		
Function	**Category**	**Subcategory**	**MIL 1**	**MIL 2**	**MIL 3**	**NERC CIP v5**
PROTECT (PR)	**Information Protection Processes and Procedures (IP):** Security policies (that address purpose, scope, roles, responsibilities, management commitment, and coordination among organizational entities), processes, and procedures are maintained and used to manage protection of information systems and assets.	**PR.IP-9:** Response plans (Incident Response and Business Continuity) and recovery plans (Incident Recovery and Disaster Recovery) are in place and managed	IR-4c	IR-3e IR-3f IR-4d IR-4f IR-5a IR-5b IR-5c IR-5d RM-1a RM-1b TVM-1d	IR-3k IR-3m IR-4i IR-4j IR-5e IR-5f IR-5g IR-5h IR-5i RM-1c	CIP-008-5 R3: Each Responsible Entity shall maintain each of its Cyber Security Incident response plans according to each of the applicable requirement parts in CIP-008-5 Table R3 – Cyber Security Incident Response Plan Review, Update, and Communication.
PROTECT (PR)	**Information Protection Processes and Procedures (IP):** Security policies (that address purpose, scope, roles, responsibilities, management commitment, and coordination among organizational entities), processes, and procedures are maintained and used to manage protection of information systems and assets.	**PR.IP-9:** Response plans (Incident Response and Business Continuity) and recovery plans (Incident Recovery and Disaster Recovery) are in place and managed	IR-4c	IR-3e IR-3f IR-4d IR-4f IR-5a IR-5b IR-5c IR-5d RM-1a RM-1b TVM-1d	IR-3k IR-3m IR-4i IR-4j IR-5e IR-5f IR-5g IR-5h IR-5i RM-1c	CIP-009-5 R1: Each Responsible Entity shall have one or more documented recovery plans that collectively include each of the applicable requirement parts in CIP-009-5 Table R1 – Recovery Plan Specifications.

Mapping of NIST Cybersecurity Framework v1.0 to NERC CIP version 5 & C2M2 Practices

Function	Category	Subcategory	C2M2 Practices **			NERC CIP v5
			MIL 1	MIL 2	MIL 3	
PROTECT (PR)	Information Protection Processes and Procedures (IP): Security policies (that address purpose, scope, roles, responsibilities, management commitment, and coordination among organizational entities), processes, and procedures are maintained and used to manage protection of information systems and assets.	PR.IP-9: Response plans (Incident Response and Business Continuity) and recovery plans (Incident Recovery and Disaster Recovery) are in place and managed	IR-4c	IR-3e IR-3f IR-4d IR-4f IR-5a IR-5b IR-5c IR-5d RM-1a RM-1b TVM-1d	IR-3k IR-3m IR-4i IR-4j IR-5e IR-5f IR-5g IR-5h IR-5i RM-1c	CIP-009-5 R3: Each Responsible Entity shall maintain each of its recovery plans in accordance with each of the applicable requirement parts in CIP-009-5 Table R3 – Recovery Plan Review, Update and Communication.
PROTECT (PR)	Information Protection Processes and Procedures (IP): Security policies (that address purpose, scope, roles, responsibilities, management commitment, and coordination among organizational entities), processes, and procedures are maintained and used to manage protection of information systems and assets.	PR.IP-10: Response and recovery plans are tested		IR-3e IR-4f	IR-3k IR-4i IR-4j	CIP-008-5 R2: Each Responsible Entity shall implement each of its documented Cyber Security Incident response plans to collectively include each of the applicable requirement parts in CIP-008-5 Table R2 – Cyber Security Incident Response Plan Implementation and Testing.
PROTECT (PR)	Information Protection Processes and Procedures (IP): Security policies (that address purpose, scope, roles, responsibilities, management commitment, and coordination among organizational entities), processes, and procedures are maintained and used to manage protection of information systems and assets.	PR.IP-10: Response and recovery plans are tested		IR-3e IR-4f	IR-3k IR-4i IR-4j	CIP-009-5 R2: Each Responsible Entity shall implement, in a manner that identifies, assesses, and corrects deficiencies, its documented recovery plan(s) to collectively include each of the applicable requirement parts in CIP-009-5 Table R2 – Recovery Plan Implementation and Testing.

| Function | Category | Subcategory | C2M2 Practices ** | | | NERC CIP v5 |
			MIL 1	MIL 2	MIL 3	
PROTECT (PR)	**Information Protection Processes and Procedures (IP):** Security policies (that address purpose, scope, roles, responsibilities, management commitment, and coordination among organizational entities), processes, and procedures are maintained and used to manage protection of information systems and assets.	**PR.IP-11:** Cybersecurity is included in human resources practices (e.g., deprovisioning, personnel screening)	WM-2a WM-2b	WM-2c WM-2d	WM-2e WM-2f WM-2g WM-2h	CIP-004-5.1 R3: Each Responsible Entity shall implement, in a manner that identifies, assesses, and corrects deficiencies, one or more documented personnel risk assessment programs to attain and retain authorized electronic or authorized unescorted physical access to BES Cyber Systems that collectively include each of the applicable requirement parts in CIP-004-5.1 Table R3 – Personnel Risk Assessment Program.
PROTECT (PR)	**Information Protection Processes and Procedures (IP):** Security policies (that address purpose, scope, roles, responsibilities, management commitment, and coordination among organizational entities), processes, and procedures are maintained and used to manage protection of information systems and assets.	**PR.IP-11:** Cybersecurity is included in human resources practices (e.g., deprovisioning, personnel screening)	WM-2a WM-2b	WM-2c WM-2d	WM-2e WM-2f WM-2g WM-2h	CIP-004-5.1 R4: Each Responsible Entity shall implement, in a manner that identifies, assesses, and corrects deficiencies, one or more documented access management programs that collectively include each of the applicable requirement parts in CIP-004-5.1 Table R4 - Access Management Program.
PROTECT (PR)	**Information Protection Processes and Procedures (IP):** Security policies (that address purpose, scope, roles, responsibilities, management commitment, and coordination among organizational entities), processes, and procedures are maintained and used to manage protection of information systems and assets.	**PR.IP-11:** Cybersecurity is included in human resources practices (e.g., deprovisioning, personnel screening)	WM-2a WM-2b	WM-2c WM-2d	WM-2e WM-2f WM-2g WM-2h	CIP-004-5.1 R5: Each Responsible Entity shall implement, in a manner that identifies, assesses, and corrects deficiencies, one or more documented access revocation programs that collectively include each of the applicable requirement parts in CIP-004-5.1 Table R5 – Access Revocation.

Mapping of NIST Cybersecurity Framework v1.0 to NERC CIP version 5 & C2M2 Practices

98

Mapping of NIST Cybersecurity Framework v1.0 to NERC CIP version 5 & C2M2 Practices

Function	Category	Subcategory	C2M2 Practices **			NERC CIP v5
			MIL 1	MIL 2	MIL 3	
PROTECT (PR)	**Information Protection Processes and Procedures (IP):** Security policies (that address purpose, scope, roles, responsibilities, management commitment, and coordination among organizational entities), processes, and procedures are maintained and used to manage protection of information systems and assets.	**PR.IP-12:** A vulnerability management plan is developed and implemented		TVM-2d TVM-2e	TVM-3e TVM-3f	CIP-007-5 R2: Each Responsible Entity shall implement, in a manner that identifies, assesses, and corrects deficiencies, one or more documented processes that collectively include each of the applicable requirement parts in CIP-007-5 Table R2 – Security Patch Management.
PROTECT (PR)	**Information Protection Processes and Procedures (IP):** Security policies (that address purpose, scope, roles, responsibilities, management commitment, and coordination among organizational entities), processes, and procedures are maintained and used to manage protection of information systems and assets.	**PR.IP-12:** A vulnerability management plan is developed and implemented		TVM-2d TVM-2e	TVM-3e TVM-3f	CIP-007-5 R3: Each Responsible Entity shall implement, in a manner that identifies, assesses, and corrects deficiencies, one or more documented processes that collectively include each of the applicable requirement parts in CIP-007-5 Table R3 – Malicious Code Prevention.
PROTECT (PR)	**Information Protection Processes and Procedures (IP):** Security policies (that address purpose, scope, roles, responsibilities, management commitment, and coordination among organizational entities), processes, and procedures are maintained and used to manage protection of information systems and assets.	**PR.IP-12:** A vulnerability management plan is developed and implemented		TVM-2d TVM-2e	TVM-3e TVM-3f	CIP-010-1 R3: Each Responsible Entity shall implement one or more documented processes that collectively include each of the applicable requirement parts in CIP-010 - 1 Table R3– Vulnerability Assessments.

Mapping of NIST Cybersecurity Framework v1.0 to NERC CIP version 5 & C2M2 Practices

Function	Category	Subcategory	C2M2 Practices **			NERC CIP v5
			MIL 1	MIL 2	MIL 3	
PROTECT (PR)	**Maintenance (MA):** Maintenance and repairs of industrial control and information system components is performed consistent with policies and procedures.	**PR.MA-1:** Maintenance and repair of organizational assets is performed and logged in a timely manner, with approved and controlled tools	IAM-2a	ACM-1c	AMC-3f	CIP-010-1 R1: Each Responsible Entity shall implement, in a manner that identifies, assesses, and corrects deficiencies, one or more documented processes that collectively include each of the applicable requirement parts in CIP-010-1 Table R1 – Configuration Change Management.
PROTECT (PR)	**Maintenance (MA):** Maintenance and repairs of industrial control and information system components is performed consistent with policies and procedures.	**PR.MA-1:** Maintenance and repair of organizational assets is performed and logged in a timely manner, with approved and controlled tools	IAM-2a	ACM-1c	AMC-3f	CIP-006-5 R3: Each Responsible Entity shall implement one or more documented Physical Access Control System maintenance and testing programs that collectively include each of the applicable requirement parts in CIP-006-5 Table R3 – Maintenance and Testing Program.
PROTECT (PR)	**Maintenance (MA):** Maintenance and repairs of industrial control and information system components is performed consistent with policies and procedures.	**PR.MA-2:** Remote maintenance of organizational assets is approved, logged, and performed in a manner that prevents unauthorized access	SA-1a IR-1c IAM-2a IAM-2b IAM-2c	IAM-2d IAM-2e IAM-2f	IAM-2g IAM-2h IAM-2i	CIP-005-5 R2: Each Responsible Entity allowing Interactive Remote Access to BES Cyber Systems shall implement one or more documented processes that collectively include the applicable requirement parts, where technically feasible, in CIP-005-5 Table R2 – Interactive Remote Access Management.
PROTECT (PR)	**Maintenance (MA):** Maintenance and repairs of industrial control and information system components is performed consistent with policies and procedures.	**PR.MA-2:** Remote maintenance of organizational assets is approved, logged, and performed in a manner that prevents unauthorized access	SA-1a IR-1c IAM-2a IAM-2b IAM-2c	IAM-2d IAM-2e IAM-2f	IAM-2g IAM-2h IAM-2i	CIP-006-5 R3: Each Responsible Entity shall implement one or more documented Physical Access Control System maintenance and testing programs that collectively include each of the applicable requirement parts in CIP-006-5 Table R3 – Maintenance and Testing Program.
PROTECT (PR)	**Maintenance (MA):** Maintenance and repairs of industrial control and information system components is performed consistent with policies and procedures.	**PR.MA-2:** Remote maintenance of organizational assets is approved, logged, and performed in a manner that prevents unauthorized access	SA-1a IR-1c IAM-2a IAM-2b	IAM-2d IAM-2e IAM-2f	IAM-2g IAM-2h IAM-2i	CIP-010-1 R1: Each Responsible Entity shall implement, in a manner that identifies, assesses, and corrects deficiencies, one or more documented processes that collectively include each of the applicable requirement parts in CIP-

Mapping of NIST Cybersecurity Framework v1.0 to NERC CIP version 5 & C2M2 Practices

Function	Category	Subcategory	C2M2 Practices ** MIL 1	MIL 2	MIL 3	NERC CIP v5
			IAM-2c			010-1 Table R1 – Configuration Change Management.
PROTECT (PR)	**Protective Technology (PT):** Technical security solutions are managed to ensure the security and resilience of systems and assets, consistent with related policies, procedures, and agreements.	**PR.PT-1**: Audit/log records are determined, documented, implemented, and reviewed in accordance with policy	SA-1a SA-2a	SA-1b SA-1c SA-2e SA-4a	SA-1d SA-1e SA-3d SA-4e	CIP-006-5 R1 - 1.6: Monitor each Physical Access Control System for unauthorized physical access to a Physical Access Control System.
PROTECT (PR)	**Protective Technology (PT):** Technical security solutions are managed to ensure the security and resilience of systems and assets, consistent with related policies, procedures, and agreements.	**PR.PT-1**: Audit/log records are determined, documented, implemented, and reviewed in accordance with policy	SA-1a SA-2a	SA-1b SA-1c SA-2e SA-4a	SA-1d SA-1e SA-3d SA-4e	CIP-006-5 R1 - 1.8: Log (through automated means or by personnel who control entry) entry of each individual with authorized unescorted physical access into each Physical Security Perimeter, with information to identify the individual and date and time of entry.
PROTECT (PR)	**Protective Technology (PT):** Technical security solutions are managed to ensure the security and resilience of systems and assets, consistent with related policies, procedures, and agreements.	**PR.PT-1**: Audit/log records are determined, documented, implemented, and reviewed in accordance with policy	SA-1a SA-2a	SA-1b SA-1c SA-2e SA-4a	SA-1d SA-1e SA-3d SA-4e	CIP-006-5 R1 - 1.9: Retain physical access logs of entry of individuals with authorized unescorted physical access into each Physical Security Perimeter for at least ninety calendar days.
PROTECT (PR)	**Protective Technology (PT):** Technical security solutions are managed to ensure the security and resilience of systems and assets, consistent with related policies, procedures, and agreements.	**PR.PT-1**: Audit/log records are determined, documented, implemented, and reviewed in accordance with policy	SA-1a SA-2a	SA-1b SA-1c SA-2e SA-4a	SA-1d SA-1e SA-3d SA-4e	CIP-006-5 R2 - 2.2: Require manual or automated logging of visitor entry into and exit from the Physical Security Perimeter that includes date and time of the initial entry and last exit, the visitor's name, and the name of an individual point of contact responsible for the visitor, except during CIP Exceptional Circumstances.

Mapping of NIST Cybersecurity Framework v1.0 to NERC CIP version 5 & C2M2 Practices

Function	Category	Subcategory	C2M2 Practices **			NERC CIP v5
			MIL 1	MIL 2	MIL 3	
PROTECT (PR)	**Protective Technology (PT):** Technical security solutions are managed to ensure the security and resilience of systems and assets, consistent with related policies, procedures, and agreements.	**PR.PT-1**: Audit/log records are determined, documented, implemented, and reviewed in accordance with policy	SA-1a SA-2a	SA-1b SA-1c SA-2e SA-4a	SA-1d SA-1e SA-3d SA-4e	CIP-006-5 R1 - 2.3: Retain visitor logs for at least ninety calendar days.
PROTECT (PR)	**Protective Technology (PT):** Technical security solutions are managed to ensure the security and resilience of systems and assets, consistent with related policies, procedures, and agreements.	**PR.PT-1**: Audit/log records are determined, documented, implemented, and reviewed in accordance with policy	SA-1a SA-2a	SA-1b SA-1c SA-2e SA-4a	SA-1d SA-1e SA-3d SA-4e	CIP-007-5 R4 - 4.3: Where technically feasible, retain applicable event logs identified in Part 4.1 for at least the last 90 consecutive calendar days except under CIP Exceptional Circumstances.
PROTECT (PR)	**Protective Technology (PT):** Technical security solutions are managed to ensure the security and resilience of systems and assets, consistent with related policies, procedures, and agreements.	**PR.PT-1**: Audit/log records are determined, documented, implemented, and reviewed in accordance with policy	SA-1a SA-2a	SA-1b SA-1c SA-2e SA-4a	SA-1d SA-1e SA-3d SA-4e	CIP-007-5 R4 - 4.4: Review a summarization or sampling of logged events as determined by the Responsible Entity at intervals no greater than 15 calendar days to identify undetected Cyber Security Incidents.
PROTECT (PR)	**Protective Technology (PT):** Technical security solutions are managed to ensure the security and resilience of systems and assets, consistent with related policies, procedures, and agreements.	**PR.PT-2**: Removable media is protected and its use restricted according to policy	IAM-2a IAM-2b IAM-1c	IAM-2c	IAM-2e IAM-3f IAM-1i	
PROTECT (PR)	**Protective Technology (PT):** Technical security solutions are managed to ensure the security and resilience of systems and assets, consistent with related policies, procedures, and agreements.	**PR.PT-3**: Access to systems and assets is controlled, incorporating the principle of least functionality	IAM-2a IAM-2b IAM-2c	IAM-2d IAM-2e IAM-2f	IAM-2g IAM-2h IAM-2i	CIP-004-5.1 R4: Each Responsible Entity shall implement, in a manner that identifies, assesses, and corrects deficiencies, one or more documented access management programs that collectively include each of the applicable requirement parts in CIP-004-5.1 Table R4 – Access Management Program.

Mapping of NIST Cybersecurity Framework v1.0 to NERC CIP version 5 & C2M2 Practices

Function	Category	Subcategory	C2M2 Practices **			NERC CIP v5
			MIL 1	MIL 2	MIL 3	
PROTECT (PR)	**Protective Technology (PT):** Technical security solutions are managed to ensure the security and resilience of systems and assets, consistent with related policies, procedures, and agreements.	**PR.PT-3:** Access to systems and assets is controlled, incorporating the principle of least functionality	IAM-2a IAM-2b IAM-2c	IAM-2d IAM-2e IAM-2f	IAM-2g IAM-2h IAM-2i	CIP-004-5.1 R5: Each Responsible Entity shall implement, in a manner that identifies, assesses, and corrects deficiencies, one or more documented access revocation programs that collectively include each of the applicable requirement parts in CIP-004-5.1 Table R5 – Access Revocation.
PROTECT (PR)	**Protective Technology (PT):** Technical security solutions are managed to ensure the security and resilience of systems and assets, consistent with related policies, procedures, and agreements.	**PR.PT-3:** Access to systems and assets is controlled, incorporating the principle of least functionality	IAM-2a IAM-2b IAM-2c	IAM-2d IAM-2e IAM-2f	IAM-2g IAM-2h IAM-2i	CIP-005-5 R2: Each Responsible Entity allowing Interactive Remote Access to BES Cyber Systems shall implement one or more documented processes that collectively include the applicable requirement parts, where technically feasible, in CIP-005-5 Table R2 – Interactive Remote Access Management.
PROTECT (PR)	**Protective Technology (PT):** Technical security solutions are managed to ensure the security and resilience of systems and assets, consistent with related policies, procedures, and agreements.	**PR.PT-3:** Access to systems and assets is controlled, incorporating the principle of least functionality	IAM-2a IAM-2b IAM-2c	IAM-2d IAM-2e IAM-2f	IAM-2g IAM-2h IAM-2i	CIP-007-5 R5: Each Responsible Entity shall implement, in a manner that identifies, assesses, and corrects deficiencies, one or more documented processes that collectively include each of the applicable requirement parts in CIP-007-5 Table R5 – System Access Controls.
PROTECT (PR)	**Protective Technology (PT):** Technical security solutions are managed to ensure the security and resilience of systems and assets, consistent with related policies, procedures, and agreements.	**PR.PT-4:** Communications and control networks are protected	CPM-3a	CPM-3b CPM-3c	CPM-3d	CIP-004-5.1 R4: Each Responsible Entity shall implement, in a manner that identifies, assesses, and corrects deficiencies, one or more documented access management programs that collectively include each of the applicable requirement parts in CIP-004-5.1 Table R4 – Access Management Program.
PROTECT (PR)	**Protective Technology (PT):** Technical security solutions are managed to ensure the security and resilience of systems and assets, consistent with related	**PR.PT-4:** Communications and control networks are protected	CPM-3a	CPM-3b CPM-3c	CPM-3d	CIP-005-5 R1: Each Responsible Entity shall implement one or more documented processes that collectively include each of the applicable requirement parts in CIP-

Mapping of NIST Cybersecurity Framework v1.0 to NERC CIP version 5 & C2M2 Practices

Function	Category	Subcategory	C2M2 Practices **			NERC CIP v5
			MIL 1	MIL 2	MIL 3	
	policies, procedures, and agreements.					005-5 Table R1 – Electronic Security Perimeter.
PROTECT (PR)	**Protective Technology (PT):** Technical security solutions are managed to ensure the security and resilience of systems and assets, consistent with related policies, procedures, and agreements.	**PR.PT-4:** Communications and control networks are protected	CPM-3a	CPM-3b CPM-3c	CPM-3d	CIP-005-5 R2: Each Responsible Entity allowing Interactive Remote Access to BES Cyber Systems shall implement one or more documented processes that collectively include the applicable requirement parts, where technically feasible, in CIP-005-5 Table R2 – Interactive Remote Access Management.
DETECT (DE)	**Anomalies and Events (AE):** Anomalous activity is detected in a timely manner and the potential impact of events is understood.	**DE.AE-1:** A baseline of network operations and expected data flows for users and systems is established and managed	SA-2b	SA-2e		
DETECT (DE)	**Anomalies and Events (AE):** Anomalous activity is detected in a timely manner and the potential impact of events is understood.	**DE.AE-2:** Detected events are analyzed to understand attack targets and methods			IR-2i IR-3h	CIP-003-5 R1 - 1.5: Each Responsible Entity, for its high impact and medium impact BES Cyber Systems, shall review and obtain CIP Senior Manager approval at least once every 15 calendar months for one or more documented cyber security policies that collectively address the following topics: Incident reporting and response planning (CIP-008);
DETECT (DE)	**Anomalies and Events (AE):** Anomalous activity is detected in a timely manner and the potential impact of events is understood.	**DE.AE-2:** Detected events are analyzed to understand attack targets and methods			IR-2i IR-3h	CIP-007-5 R4: Each Responsible Entity shall implement, in a manner that identifies, assesses, and corrects deficiencies, one or more documented processes that collectively include each of the applicable requirement parts in CIP-007-5 Table R4 – Security Event Monitoring.

Mapping of NIST Cybersecurity Framework v1.0 to NERC CIP version 5 & C2M2 Practices

Function	Category	Subcategory	C2M2 Practices **			NERC CIP v5
			MIL 1	MIL 2	MIL 3	
DETECT (DE)	**Anomalies and Events (AE):** Anomalous activity is detected in a timely manner and the potential impact of events is understood.	**DE.AE-2:** Detected events are analyzed to understand attack targets and methods			IR-2i IR-3h	CIP-008-5 R1: Each Responsible Entity shall document one or more Cyber Security Incident response plan(s) that collectively include each of the applicable requirement parts in CIP-008-5 Table R1 – Cyber Security Incident Response Plan Specifications.
DETECT (DE)	**Anomalies and Events (AE):** Anomalous activity is detected in a timely manner and the potential impact of events is understood.	**DE.AE-2:** Detected events are analyzed to understand attack targets and methods			IR-2i IR-3h	CIP-008-5 R2: Each Responsible Entity shall implement each of its documented Cyber Security Incident response plans to collectively include each of the applicable requirement parts in CIP-008-5 Table R2 – Cyber Security Incident Response Plan Implementation and Testing.
DETECT (DE)	**Anomalies and Events (AE):** Anomalous activity is detected in a timely manner and the potential impact of events is understood.	**DE.AE-3:** Event data are aggregated and correlated from multiple sources and sensors		IR-1e	IR-1f IR-2i	CIP-007-5 R4: Each Responsible Entity shall implement, in a manner that identifies, assesses, and corrects deficiencies, one or more documented processes that collectively include each of the applicable requirement parts in CIP-007-5 Table R4 – Security Event Monitoring.
DETECT (DE)	**Anomalies and Events (AE):** Anomalous activity is detected in a timely manner and the potential impact of events is understood.	**DE.AE-4:** Impact of events is determined	IR-2b	IR-2d	IR-2g	CIP-008-5 R1 - 1.1: Each Responsible Entity shall document one or more Cyber Security Incident response plan(s) that collectively include 1.1 One or more processes to identify, classify, and respond to Cyber Security Incidents.
DETECT (DE)	**Anomalies and Events (AE):** Anomalous activity is detected in a timely manner and the potential impact of events is understood.	**DE.AE-5:** Incident alert thresholds are established		IR-2d TVM-1d SA-2d	IR-2g RM-2j	CIP-003-5 R1 - 1.5: Each Responsible Entity, for its high impact and medium impact BES Cyber Systems, shall review and obtain CIP Senior Manager approval at least once every 15 calendar months for one or more documented cyber security policies that collectively address the

Mapping of NIST Cybersecurity Framework v1.0 to NERC CIP version 5 & C2M2 Practices

Function	Category	Subcategory	C2M2 Practices **			NERC CIP v5
			MIL 1	MIL 2	MIL 3	
						following topics: Incident reporting and response planning (CIP-008);
DETECT (DE)	**Anomalies and Events (AE):** Anomalous activity is detected in a timely manner and the potential impact of events is understood.	**DE.AE-5:** Incident alert thresholds are established		IR-2d TVM-1d SA-2d	IR-2g RM-2j	CIP-003-5 R2 - 2.4: Each Responsible Entity for its assets identified in CIP-002-5, Requirement R1, Part R1.3, shall implement, in a manner that identifies, assesses, and corrects deficiencies, one or more documented cyber security policies that collectively address the following topics, and review and obtain CIP Senior Manager approval for those policies at least once every 15 calendar months: (An inventory, list, or discrete identification of low impact BES Cyber Systems or their BES Cyber Assets is not required). Incident response to a Cyber Security Incident.
DETECT (DE)	**Anomalies and Events (AE):** Anomalous activity is detected in a timely manner and the potential impact of events is understood.	**DE.AE-5:** Incident alert thresholds are established		IR-2d TVM-1d SA-2d	IR-2g RM-2j	CIP-008-5 R1: Each Responsible Entity shall document one or more Cyber Security Incident response plan(s) that collectively include each of the applicable requirement parts in CIP-008-5 Table R1 – Cyber Security Incident Response Plan Specifications.
DETECT (DE)	**Anomalies and Events (AE):** Anomalous activity is detected in a timely manner and the potential impact of events is understood.	**DE.AE-5:** Incident alert thresholds are established		IR-2d TVM-1d SA-2d	IR-2g RM-2j	CIP-008-5 R2: Each Responsible Entity shall implement each of its documented Cyber Security Incident response plans to collectively include each of the applicable requirement parts in CIP-008-5 Table R2 – Cyber Security Incident Response Plan Implementation and Testing.

Mapping of NIST Cybersecurity Framework v1.0 to NERC CIP version 5 & C2M2 Practices

Function	Category	Subcategory	C2M2 Practices **			NERC CIP v5
			MIL 1	MIL 2	MIL 3	
DETECT (DE)	**Anomalies and Events (AE):** Anomalous activity is detected in a timely manner and the potential impact of events is understood.	**DE.AE-5:** Incident alert thresholds are established		IR-2d TVM-1d SA-2d	IR-2g RM-2j	CIP-008-5 R3: Each Responsible Entity shall maintain each of its Cyber Security Incident response plans according to each of the applicable requirement parts in CIP-008-5 Table R3 – Cyber Security Incident Response Plan Review, Update, and Communication.
DETECT (DE)	**Security Continuous Monitoring (CM):** The information system and assets are monitored at discrete intervals to identify cybersecurity events and verify the effectiveness of protective measures.	**DE.CM-1:** The network is monitored to detect potential cybersecurity events	SA-2a SA-2b	SA-2e SA-2f	SA-2g SA-2i	CIP-005-5 R1 - 1.5: Each Responsible Entity shall implement one or more documented processes that collectively include each of the applicable requirement parts in CIP-005-5 Table R1 – Electronic Security Perimeter. Have one or more methods for detecting known or suspected malicious communications for both inbound and outbound communications.
DETECT (DE)	**Security Continuous Monitoring (CM):** The information system and assets are monitored at discrete intervals to identify cybersecurity events and verify the effectiveness of protective measures.	**DE.CM-2:** The physical environment is monitored to detect potential cybersecurity events	SA-2a SA-2b		SA-2i	CIP-006-5 R1: Each Responsible Entity shall implement, in a manner that identifies, assesses, and corrects deficiencies, one or more documented physical security plans that collectively include all of the applicable requirement parts in CIP-006-5 Table R1 – Physical Security Plan.
DETECT (DE)	**Security Continuous Monitoring (CM):** The information system and assets are monitored at discrete intervals to identify cybersecurity events and verify the effectiveness of protective measures.	**DE.CM-2:** The physical environment is monitored to detect potential cybersecurity events	SA-2a SA-2b		SA-2i	CIP-006-5 R2: Each Responsible Entity shall implement, in a manner that identifies, assesses, and corrects deficiencies, one or more documented visitor control programs that include each of the applicable requirement parts in CIP-006-5 Table R2 – Visitor Control Program.

Mapping of NIST Cybersecurity Framework v1.0 to NERC CIP version 5 & C2M2 Practices

Function	Category	Subcategory	C2M2 Practices **			NERC CIP v5
			MIL 1	MIL 2	MIL 3	
DETECT (DE)	**Security Continuous Monitoring (CM):** The information system and assets are monitored at discrete intervals to identify cybersecurity events and verify the effectiveness of protective measures.	**DE.CM-3:** Personnel activity is monitored to detect potential cybersecurity events	SA-2a SA-2b		SA-2i	CIP-003-5 R1 - 1.2: Each Responsible Entity, for its high impact and medium impact BES Cyber Systems, shall review and obtain CIP Senior Manager approval at least once every 15 calendar months for one or more documented cyber security policies that collectively address the following topics: Electronic Security Perimeters (CIP-005) including Interactive Remote Access;
DETECT (DE)	**Security Continuous Monitoring (CM):** The information system and assets are monitored at discrete intervals to identify cybersecurity events and verify the effectiveness of protective measures.	**DE.CM-3:** Personnel activity is monitored to detect potential cybersecurity events	SA-2a SA-2b		SA-2i	CIP-003-5 R1 - 1.4: Each Responsible Entity, for its high impact and medium impact BES Cyber Systems, shall review and obtain CIP Senior Manager approval at least once every 15 calendar months for one or more documented cyber security policies that collectively address the following topics: System security management (CIP-007);
DETECT (DE)	**Security Continuous Monitoring (CM):** The information system and assets are monitored at discrete intervals to identify cybersecurity events and verify the effectiveness of protective measures.	**DE.CM-3:** Personnel activity is monitored to detect potential cybersecurity events	SA-2a SA-2b		SA-2i	CIP-007-5 R4: Each Responsible Entity shall implement, in a manner that identifies, assesses, and corrects deficiencies, one or more documented processes that collectively include each of the applicable requirement parts in CIP-007-5 Table R4 – Security Event Monitoring.
DETECT (DE)	**Security Continuous Monitoring (CM):** The information system and assets are monitored at discrete intervals to identify cybersecurity events and verify the effectiveness of protective measures.	**DE.CM-3:** Personnel activity is monitored to detect potential cybersecurity events	SA-2a SA-2b		SA-2i	CIP-007-5 R5: Each Responsible Entity shall implement, in a manner that identifies, assesses, and corrects deficiencies, one or more documented processes that collectively include each of the applicable requirement parts in CIP-007-5 Table R5 – System Access Controls.

Mapping of NIST Cybersecurity Framework v1.0 to NERC CIP version 5 & C2M2 Practices

Function	Category	Subcategory	C2M2 Practices **			NERC CIP v5
			MIL 1	MIL 2	MIL 3	
DETECT (DE)	**Security Continuous Monitoring (CM):** The information system and assets are monitored at discrete intervals to identify cybersecurity events and verify the effectiveness of protective measures.	**DE.CM-4:** Malicious code is detected	SA-2a SA-2b	SA-2e CPM-4a	SA-2i	CIP-003-5 R1 - 1.2: Each Responsible Entity, for its high impact and medium impact BES Cyber Systems, shall review and obtain CIP Senior Manager approval at least once every 15 calendar months for one or more documented cyber security policies that collectively address the following topics: Electronic Security Perimeters (CIP-005) including Interactive Remote Access;
DETECT (DE)	**Security Continuous Monitoring (CM):** The information system and assets are monitored at discrete intervals to identify cybersecurity events and verify the effectiveness of protective measures.	**DE.CM-4:** Malicious code is detected	SA-2a SA-2b	SA-2e CPM-4a	SA-2i	CIP-007-5 R3: Each Responsible Entity shall implement, in a manner that identifies, assesses, and corrects deficiencies, one or more documented processes that collectively include each of the applicable requirement parts in CIP-007-5 Table R3 – Malicious Code Prevention.
DETECT (DE)	**Security Continuous Monitoring (CM):** The information system and assets are monitored at discrete intervals to identify cybersecurity events and verify the effectiveness of protective measures.	**DE.CM-5:** Unauthorized mobile code is detected	SA-2a SA-2b	SA-2e	SA-2h SA-2i	CIP-007-5 R3: Each Responsible Entity shall implement, in a manner that identifies, assesses, and corrects deficiencies, one or more documented processes that collectively include each of the applicable requirement parts in CIP-007-5 Table R3 – Malicious Code Prevention.
DETECT (DE)	**Security Continuous Monitoring (CM):** The information system and assets are monitored at discrete intervals to identify cybersecurity events and verify the effectiveness of protective measures.	**DE.CM-5:** Unauthorized mobile code is detected	SA-2a SA-2b	SA-2e	SA-2h SA-2i	CIP-010-1 R2: Each Responsible Entity shall implement, in a manner that identifies, assesses, and corrects deficiencies, one or more documented processes that collectively include each of the applicable requirement parts in CIP-010-1 Table R2 – Configuration Monitoring.

Mapping of NIST Cybersecurity Framework v1.0 to NERC CIP version 5 & C2M2 Practices

Function	Category	Subcategory	C2M2 Practices **			NERC CIP v5
			MIL 1	MIL 2	MIL 3	
DETECT (DE)	**Security Continuous Monitoring (CM):** The information system and assets are monitored at discrete intervals to identify cybersecurity events and verify the effectiveness of protective measures.	**DE.CM-6:** External service provider activity is monitored to detect potential cybersecurity events	EDM-2a SA-2a SA-2b		EDM-2j EDM-2l EDM-2n	CIP-005-5 R1 - 1.5: Each Responsible Entity shall implement one or more documented processes that collectively include each of the applicable requirement parts in CIP-005-5 Table R1 – Electronic Security Perimeter. Have one or more methods for detecting known or suspected malicious communications for both inbound and outbound communications.
DETECT (DE)	**Security Continuous Monitoring (CM):** The information system and assets are monitored at discrete intervals to identify cybersecurity events and verify the effectiveness of protective measures.	**DE.CM-7:** Monitoring for unauthorized personnel, connections, devices, and software is performed	SA-2a SA-2b	SA-2e SA-2f	SA-2g SA-2i	CIP-003-5 R2 - 2.3: Each Responsible Entity for its assets identified in CIP-002-5, Requirement R1, Part R1.3, shall implement, in a manner that identifies, assesses, and corrects deficiencies, one or more documented cyber security policies that collectively address the following topics, and review and obtain CIP Senior Manager approval for those policies at least once every 15 calendar months: (An inventory, list, or discrete identification of low impact BES Cyber Systems or their BES Cyber Assets is not required). Electronic access controls for external routable protocol connections and Dial-up Connectivity;
DETECT (DE)	**Security Continuous Monitoring (CM):** The information system and assets are monitored at discrete intervals to identify cybersecurity events and verify the effectiveness of protective measures.	**DE.CM-7:** Monitoring for unauthorized personnel, connections, devices, and software is performed	SA-2a SA-2b	SA-2e SA-2f	SA-2g SA-2i	CIP-004-5.1 R3: Each Responsible Entity shall implement, in a manner that identifies, assesses, and corrects deficiencies, one or more documented personnel risk assessment programs to attain and retain authorized electronic or authorized unescorted physical access to BES Cyber Systems that collectively include each of the applicable requirement parts in CIP-004-5.1 Table R3 – Personnel Risk Assessment Program.

Mapping of NIST Cybersecurity Framework v1.0 to NERC CIP version 5 & C2M2 Practices

Function	Category	Subcategory	C2M2 Practices **			NERC CIP v5
			MIL 1	MIL 2	MIL 3	
DETECT (DE)	Security Continuous Monitoring (CM): The information system and assets are monitored at discrete intervals to identify cybersecurity events and verify the effectiveness of protective measures.	DE.CM-7: Monitoring for unauthorized personnel, connections, devices, and software is performed	SA-2a SA-2b	SA-2e SA-2f	SA-2g SA-2i	CIP-006-5 R1 - 1.5: Issue an alarm or alert in response to detected unauthorized access through a physical access point into a Physical Security Perimeter to the personnel identified in the BES Cyber Security Incident response plan within 15 minutes of detection.
DETECT (DE)	Security Continuous Monitoring (CM): The information system and assets are monitored at discrete intervals to identify cybersecurity events and verify the effectiveness of protective measures.	DE.CM-7: Monitoring for unauthorized personnel, connections, devices, and software is performed	SA-2a SA-2b	SA-2e SA-2f	SA-2g SA-2i	CIP-006-5 R1 - 1.6: Monitor each Physical Access Control System for unauthorized physical access to a Physical Access Control System.
DETECT (DE)	Security Continuous Monitoring (CM): The information system and assets are monitored at discrete intervals to identify cybersecurity events and verify the effectiveness of protective measures.	DE.CM-7: Monitoring for unauthorized personnel, connections, devices, and software is performed	SA-2a SA-2b	SA-2e SA-2f	SA-2g SA-2i	CIP-007-5 R4: Each Responsible Entity shall implement, in a manner that identifies, assesses, and corrects deficiencies, one or more documented processes that collectively include each of the applicable requirement parts in CIP-007-5 Table R4 – Security Event Monitoring.
DETECT (DE)	Security Continuous Monitoring (CM): The information system and assets are monitored at discrete intervals to identify cybersecurity events and verify the effectiveness of protective measures.	DE.CM-8: Vulnerability scans are performed		TVM-2e	TVM-2i	CIP-003-5 R1 - 1.7: Each Responsible Entity, for its high impact and medium impact BES Cyber Systems, shall review and obtain CIP Senior Manager approval at least once every 15 calendar months for one or more documented cyber security policies that collectively address the following topics: Configuration change management and vulnerability assessments (CIP-010);
DETECT (DE)	Security Continuous Monitoring (CM): The information system and assets are monitored at discrete intervals to identify cybersecurity events and verify the effectiveness of protective measures.	DE.CM-8: Vulnerability scans are performed		TVM-2e	TVM-2i	CIP-007-5 R3: Each Responsible Entity shall implement, in a manner that identifies, assesses, and corrects deficiencies, one or more documented processes that collectively include each of the applicable requirement parts in CIP-

Mapping of NIST Cybersecurity Framework v1.0 to NERC CIP version 5 & C2M2 Practices

Function	Category	Subcategory	C2M2 Practices **			NERC CIP v5
			MIL 1	MIL 2	MIL 3	
						007-5 Table R3 – Malicious Code Prevention.
DETECT (DE)	**Security Continuous Monitoring (CM):** The information system and assets are monitored at discrete intervals to identify cybersecurity events and verify the effectiveness of protective measures.	**DE.CM-8:** Vulnerability scans are performed		TVM-2e	TVM-2i	CIP-010-1 R3: Each Responsible Entity shall implement one or more documented processes that collectively include each of the applicable requirement parts in CIP - 010 - 1 Table R3– Vulnerability Assessments.
DETECT (DE)	**Detection Processes (DP):** Detection Processes (DP): Detection processes and procedures are maintained and tested to ensure timely and adequate awareness of anomalous events.	**DE.DP-1:** Roles and responsibilities for detection are well defined to ensure accountability	IR-1a IR-3a WM-1a WM-1b	WM-1d	WM-1f WM-1h	CIP-003-5 R1 - 1.1: Each Responsible Entity, for its high impact and medium impact BES Cyber Systems, shall review and obtain CIP Senior Manager approval at least once every 15 calendar months for one or more documented cyber security policies that collectively address the following topics: Personnel & training (CIP-004)
DETECT (DE)	**Detection Processes (DP):** Detection Processes (DP): Detection processes and procedures are maintained and tested to ensure timely and adequate awareness of anomalous events.	**DE.DP-1:** Roles and responsibilities for detection are well defined to ensure accountability	IR-1a IR-3a WM-1a WM-1b	WM-1d	WM-1f WM-1h	CIP-003-5 R3: Each Responsible Entity shall identify a CIP Senior Manager by name and document any change within 30 calendar days of the change.

Mapping of NIST Cybersecurity Framework v1.0 to NERC CIP version 5 & C2M2 Practices

Function	Category	Subcategory	C2M2 Practices **			NERC CIP v5
			MIL 1	MIL 2	MIL 3	
DETECT (DE)	**Detection Processes (DP):** Detection Processes (DP): Detection processes and procedures are maintained and tested to ensure timely and adequate awareness of anomalous events.	**DE.DP-1:** Roles and responsibilities for detection are well defined to ensure accountability	IR-1a IR-3a WM-1a WM-1b	WM-1d	WM-1f WM-1h	CIP-003-5 R4: The Responsible Entity shall implement, in a manner that identifies, assesses, and corrects deficiencies, a documented process to delegate authority, unless no delegations are used. Where allowed by the CIP Standards, the CIP Senior Manager may delegate authority for specific actions to a delegate or delegates. These delegations shall be documented, including the name or title of the delegate, the specific actions delegated, and the date of the delegation; approved by the CIP Senior Manager; and updated within 30 days of any change to the delegation. Delegation changes do not need to be reinstated with a change to the delegator.
DETECT (DE)	**Detection Processes (DP):** Detection Processes (DP): Detection processes and procedures are maintained and tested to ensure timely and adequate awareness of anomalous events.	**DE.DP-1:** Roles and responsibilities for detection are well defined to ensure accountability	IR-1a IR-3a WM-1a WM-1b	WM-1d	WM-1f WM-1h	CIP-007-5 R3: Each Responsible Entity shall implement, in a manner that identifies, assesses, and corrects deficiencies, one or more documented processes that collectively include each of the applicable requirement parts in CIP-007-5 Table R3 – Malicious Code Prevention.
DETECT (DE)	**Detection Processes (DP):** Detection Processes (DP): Detection processes and procedures are maintained and tested to ensure timely and adequate awareness of anomalous events.	**DE.DP-1:** Roles and responsibilities for detection are well defined to ensure accountability	IR-1a IR-3a WM-1a WM-1b	WM-1d	WM-1f WM-1h	CIP-008-5 R1: Each Responsible Entity shall document one or more Cyber Security Incident response plan(s) that collectively include each of the applicable requirement parts in CIP-008-5 Table R1 – Cyber Security Incident Response Plan Specifications.

Mapping of NIST Cybersecurity Framework v1.0 to NERC CIP version 5 & C2M2 Practices

Function	Category	Subcategory	C2M2 Practices **			NERC CIP v5
			MIL 1	MIL 2	MIL 3	
DETECT (DE)	**Detection Processes (DP):** Detection Processes (DP): Detection processes and procedures are maintained and tested to ensure timely and adequate awareness of anomalous events.	**DE.DP-2:** Detection activities comply with all applicable requirements		IR-1d	IR-1g IR-5f RM-1c RM-2j	CIP-008-5 R3: Each Responsible Entity shall maintain each of its Cyber Security Incident response plans according to each of the applicable requirement parts in CIP-008-5 Table R3 – Cyber Security Incident Response Plan Review, Update, and Communication.
DETECT (DE)	**Detection Processes (DP):** Detection Processes (DP): Detection processes and procedures are maintained and tested to ensure timely and adequate awareness of anomalous events.	**DE.DP-3:** Detection processes are tested		IR-3e	IR-3j	CIP-004-5.1 R2 - 2.1: Each Responsible Entity shall implement, in a manner that identifies, assesses, and corrects deficiencies, a cyber security training program(s) appropriate to individual roles, functions, or responsibilities that collectively includes each of the applicable requirement parts in CIP-004-5.1 Table R2 – Cyber Security Training Program. Training content on: 2.1.1. Cyber security policies; 2.1.2. Physical access controls; 2.1.3. Electronic access controls; 2.1.4. The visitor control program; 2.1.5. Handling of BES Cyber System Information and its storage; 2.1.6. Identification of a Cyber Security Incident and initial notifications in accordance with the entity's incident response plan; 2.1.7. Recovery plans for BES Cyber Systems; 2.1.8. Response to Cyber Security Incidents; and 2.1.9. Cyber security risks associated with a BES Cyber System's electronic interconnectivity and interoperability with other Cyber Assets.

Mapping of NIST Cybersecurity Framework v1.0 to NERC CIP version 5 & C2M2 Practices

Function	Category	Subcategory	C2M2 Practices **			NERC CIP v5
			MIL 1	MIL 2	MIL 3	
DETECT (DE)	**Detection Processes (DP):** Detection Processes (DP): Detection processes and procedures are maintained and tested to ensure timely and adequate awareness of anomalous events.	**DE.DP-3:** Detection processes are tested		IR-3e	IR-3j	CIP-006-5 R3: Each Responsible Entity shall implement one or more documented Physical Access Control System maintenance and testing programs that collectively include each of the applicable requirement parts in CIP-006-5 Table R3 – Maintenance and Testing Program.
DETECT (DE)	**Detection Processes (DP):** Detection Processes (DP): Detection processes and procedures are maintained and tested to ensure timely and adequate awareness of anomalous events.	**DE.DP-3:** Detection processes are tested		IR-3e	IR-3j	CIP-008-5 R2: Each Responsible Entity shall implement each of its documented Cyber Security Incident response plans to collectively include each of the applicable requirement parts in CIP-008-5 Table R2 – Cyber Security Incident Response Plan Implementation and Testing.
DETECT (DE)	**Detection Processes (DP):** Detection Processes (DP): Detection processes and procedures are maintained and tested to ensure timely and adequate awareness of anomalous events.	**DE.DP-4:** Event detection information is communicated to appropriate parties	IR-1b IR-3c ISC-1a	ISC-1c ISC-1d	IR-3n ISC-1h	CIP-003-5 R1 - 1.5: Each Responsible Entity, for its high impact and medium impact BES Cyber Systems, shall review and obtain CIP Senior Manager approval at least once every 15 calendar months for one or more documented cyber security policies that collectively address the following topics: Incident reporting and response planning (CIP-008);
DETECT (DE)	**Detection Processes (DP):** Detection Processes (DP): Detection processes and procedures are maintained and tested to ensure timely and adequate awareness of anomalous events.	**DE.DP-4:** Event detection information is communicated to appropriate parties	IR-1b IR-3c ISC-1a	ISC-1c ISC-1d	IR-3n ISC-1h	CIP-007-5 R4: Each Responsible Entity shall implement, in a manner that identifies, assesses, and corrects deficiencies, one or more documented processes that collectively include each of the applicable requirement parts in CIP-007-5 Table R4 – Security Event Monitoring.
DETECT (DE)	**Detection Processes (DP):** Detection Processes (DP): Detection processes and procedures are maintained and tested to ensure timely and	**DE.DP-4:** Event detection information is communicated to appropriate parties	IR-1b IR-3c ISC-1a	ISC-1c ISC-1d	IR-3n ISC-1h	CIP-008-5 R2: Each Responsible Entity shall implement each of its documented Cyber Security Incident response plans to collectively include each of the applicable requirement parts in CIP-008-5 Table R2 –

Mapping of NIST Cybersecurity Framework v1.0 to NERC CIP version 5 & C2M2 Practices

Function	Category	Subcategory	C2M2 Practices **			NERC CIP v5
			MIL 1	MIL 2	MIL 3	
	adequate awareness of anomalous events.					Cyber Security Incident Response Plan Implementation and Testing.
DETECT (DE)	**Detection Processes (DP):** Detection Processes (DP): Detection processes and procedures are maintained and tested to ensure timely and adequate awareness of anomalous events.	**DE.DP-5:** Detection processes are continuously improved		IR-3h	IR-3k	CIP-008-5 R2: Each Responsible Entity shall implement each of its documented Cyber Security Incident response plans to collectively include each of the applicable requirement parts in CIP-008-5 Table R2 – Cyber Security Incident Response Plan Implementation and Testing.
RESPOND (RS)	**Response Planning (RP):** Response processes and procedures are executed and maintained, to ensure timely response to detected cybersecurity events.	**RS.RP-1:** Response plan is executed during or after an event		IR-3d		CIP-008-5 R2: Each Responsible Entity shall implement each of its documented Cyber Security Incident response plans to collectively include each of the applicable requirement parts in CIP-008-5 Table R2 – Cyber Security Incident Response Plan Implementation and Testing.
RESPOND (RS)	**Communications (CO):** Response activities are coordinated with internal and external stakeholders, as appropriate, to include external support from law enforcement agencies.	**RS.CO-1:** Personnel know their roles and order of operations when a response is needed	IR-3a		IR-5a IR-5b	CIP-004-5.1 R2 - Part 2.1.8: Each Responsible Entity shall implement, in a manner that identifies, assesses, and corrects deficiencies, a cyber security training program(s) appropriate to individual roles, functions, or responsibilities that collectively includes each of the applicable requirement parts in CIP-004-5.1 Table R2 – Cyber Security Training Program. 2.1.8. Training content on: Response to Cyber Security Incidents;
RESPOND (RS)	**Communications (CO):** Response activities are coordinated with internal and external stakeholders, as appropriate, to include external	**RS.CO-1:** Personnel know their roles and order of operations when a response is needed	IR-3a		IR-5a IR-5b	CIP-008-5 R1: Each Responsible Entity shall document one or more Cyber Security Incident response plan(s) that collectively include each of the applicable requirement parts in CIP-008-5 Table R1 –

Mapping of NIST Cybersecurity Framework v1.0 to NERC CIP version 5 & C2M2 Practices

Function	Category	Subcategory	C2M2 Practices **			NERC CIP v5
			MIL 1	MIL 2	MIL 3	
	support from law enforcement agencies.					Cyber Security Incident Response Plan Specifications.
RESPOND (RS)	**Communications (CO):** Response activities are coordinated with internal and external stakeholders, as appropriate, to include external support from law enforcement agencies.	**RS.CO-1:** Personnel know their roles and order of operations when a response is needed	**IR-3a**		**IR-5a** **IR-5b**	CIP-008-5 R3: Each Responsible Entity shall maintain each of its Cyber Security Incident response plans according to each of the applicable requirement parts in CIP-008-5 Table R3 – Cyber Security Incident Response Plan Review, Update, and Communication.
RESPOND (RS)	**Communications (CO):** Response activities are coordinated with internal and external stakeholders, as appropriate, to include external support from law enforcement agencies.	**RS.CO-2:** Events are reported consistent with established criteria	**IR-1a** **IR-1b**			CIP-003-5 R1 - 1.5: Each Responsible Entity, for its high impact and medium impact BES Cyber Systems, shall review and obtain CIP Senior Manager approval at least once every 15 calendar months for one or more documented cyber security policies that collectively address the following topics: Incident reporting and response planning (CIP-008);
RESPOND (RS)	**Communications (CO):** Response activities are coordinated with internal and external stakeholders, as appropriate, to include external support from law enforcement agencies.	**RS.CO-2:** Events are reported consistent with established criteria	**IR-1a** **IR-1b**			CIP-003-5 R2 - 2.4: Each Responsible Entity for its assets identified in CIP-002-5, Requirement R1, Part R1.3, shall implement, in a manner that identifies, assesses, and corrects deficiencies, one or more documented cyber security policies that collectively address the following topics, and review and obtain CIP Senior Manager approval for those policies at least once every 15 calendar months: (An inventory, list, or discrete identification of low impact BES Cyber Systems or their BES Cyber Assets is not required). Incident response to a Cyber Security Incident.

Mapping of NIST Cybersecurity Framework v1.0 to NERC CIP version 5 & C2M2 Practices

Function	Category	Subcategory	C2M2 Practices **			NERC CIP v5
			MIL 1	MIL 2	MIL 3	
RESPOND (RS)	**Communications (CO):** Response activities are coordinated with internal and external stakeholders, as appropriate, to include external support from law enforcement agencies.	**RS.CO-2:** Events are reported consistent with established criteria	**IR-1a** **IR-1b**			CIP-005-5 R1 - 1.5: Each Responsible Entity shall implement one or more documented processes that collectively include each of the applicable requirement parts in CIP-005-5 Table R1 – Electronic Security Perimeter. Have one or more methods for detecting known or suspected malicious communications for both inbound and outbound communications.
RESPOND (RS)	**Communications (CO):** Response activities are coordinated with internal and external stakeholders, as appropriate, to include external support from law enforcement agencies.	**RS.CO-2:** Events are reported consistent with established criteria	**IR-1a** **IR-1b**			CIP-006-5 R1 - 1.5: Issue an alarm or alert in response to detected unauthorized access through a physical access point into a Physical Security Perimeter to the personnel identified in the BES Cyber Security Incident response plan within 15 minutes of detection.
RESPOND (RS)	**Communications (CO):** Response activities are coordinated with internal and external stakeholders, as appropriate, to include external support from law enforcement agencies.	**RS.CO-2:** Events are reported consistent with established criteria	**IR-1a** **IR-1b**			CIP-006-5 R1 - 1.7: Issue an alarm or alert in response to detected unauthorized physical access to a Physical Access Control System to the personnel identified in the BES Cyber Security Incident response plan within 15 minutes of the detection.
RESPOND (RS)	**Communications (CO):** Response activities are coordinated with internal and external stakeholders, as appropriate, to include external support from law enforcement agencies.	**RS.CO-2:** Events are reported consistent with established criteria	**IR-1a** **IR-1b**			CIP-007-5 R4: Each Responsible Entity shall implement, in a manner that identifies, assesses, and corrects deficiencies, one or more documented processes that collectively include each of the applicable requirement parts in CIP-007-5 Table R4 – Security Event Monitoring.
RESPOND (RS)	**Communications (CO):** Response activities are coordinated with internal and external stakeholders, as appropriate, to include external	**RS.CO-2:** Events are reported consistent with established criteria	**IR-1a** **IR-1b**			CIP-008-5 R1: Each Responsible Entity shall document one or more Cyber Security Incident response plan(s) that collectively include each of the applicable requirement parts in CIP-008-5 Table R1 –

118

Mapping of NIST Cybersecurity Framework v1.0 to NERC CIP version 5 & C2M2 Practices

Function	Category	Subcategory	C2M2 Practices **			NERC CIP v5
			MIL 1	MIL 2	MIL 3	
	support from law enforcement agencies.					Cyber Security Incident Response Plan Specifications.
RESPOND (RS)	**Communications (CO):** Response activities are coordinated with internal and external stakeholders, as appropriate, to include external support from law enforcement agencies.	**RS.CO-2:** Events are reported consistent with established criteria	IR-1a IR-1b			CIP-008-5 R2: Each Responsible Entity shall implement each of its documented Cyber Security Incident response plans to collectively include each of the applicable requirement parts in CIP-008-5 Table R2 – Cyber Security Incident Response Plan Implementation and Testing.
RESPOND (RS)	**Communications (CO):** Response activities are coordinated with internal and external stakeholders, as appropriate, to include external support from law enforcement agencies.	**RS.CO-2:** Events are reported consistent with established criteria	IR-1a IR-1b			CIP-008-5 R3: Each Responsible Entity shall maintain each of its Cyber Security Incident response plans according to each of the applicable requirement parts in CIP-008-5 Table R3 – Cyber Security Incident Response Plan Review, Update, and Communication.
RESPOND (RS)	**Communications (CO):** Response activities are coordinated with internal and external stakeholders, as appropriate, to include external support from law enforcement agencies.	**RS.CO-3:** Information is shared consistent with response plans	ISC-1a ISC-1b	IR-3d ISC-1c ISC-1d		CIP-008-5 R1: Each Responsible Entity shall document one or more Cyber Security Incident response plan(s) that collectively include each of the applicable requirement parts in CIP-008-5 Table R1 – Cyber Security Incident Response Plan Specifications.
RESPOND (RS)	**Communications (CO):** Response activities are coordinated with internal and external stakeholders, as appropriate, to include external support from law enforcement agencies.	**RS.CO-3:** Information is shared consistent with response plans	ISC-1a ISC-1b	IR-3d ISC-1c ISC-1d		CIP-008-5 R2: Each Responsible Entity shall implement each of its documented Cyber Security Incident response plans to collectively include each of the applicable requirement parts in CIP-008-5 Table R2 – Cyber Security Incident Response Plan Implementation and Testing.

Mapping of NIST Cybersecurity Framework v1.0 to NERC CIP version 5 & C2M2 Practices

Function	Category	Subcategory	C2M2 Practices **			NERC CIP v5
			MIL 1	MIL 2	MIL 3	
RESPOND (RS)	Communications (CO): Response activities are coordinated with internal and external stakeholders, as appropriate, to include external support from law enforcement agencies.	RS.CO-4: Coordination with stakeholders occurs consistent with response plans		IR-3d IR-5b		CIP-003-5 R2 - 2.4: Each Responsible Entity for its assets identified in CIP-002-5, Requirement R1, Part R1.3, shall implement, in a manner that identifies, assesses, and corrects deficiencies, one or more documented cyber security policies that collectively address the following topics, and review and obtain CIP Senior Manager approval for those policies at least once every 15 calendar months: (An inventory, list, or discrete identification of low impact BES Cyber Systems or their BES Cyber Assets is not required). Incident response to a Cyber Security Incident.
RESPOND (RS)	Communications (CO): Response activities are coordinated with internal and external stakeholders, as appropriate, to include external support from law enforcement agencies.	RS.CO-4: Coordination with stakeholders occurs consistent with response plans		IR-3d IR-5b		CIP-008-5 R1: Each Responsible Entity shall document one or more Cyber Security Incident response plan(s) that collectively include each of the applicable requirement parts in CIP-008-5 Table R1 – Cyber Security Incident Response Plan Specifications.
RESPOND (RS)	Communications (CO): Response activities are coordinated with internal and external stakeholders, as appropriate, to include external support from law enforcement agencies.	RS.CO-4: Coordination with stakeholders occurs consistent with response plans		IR-3d IR-5b		CIP-008-5 R2: Each Responsible Entity shall implement each of its documented Cyber Security Incident response plans to collectively include each of the applicable requirement parts in CIP-008-5 Table R2 – Cyber Security Incident Response Plan Implementation and Testing.
RESPOND (RS)	Communications (CO): Response activities are coordinated with internal and external stakeholders, as appropriate, to include external support from law enforcement agencies.	RS.CO-5: Voluntary information sharing occurs with external stakeholders to achieve broader cybersecurity situational awareness	ISC-1a ISC-1b IR-3c	ISC-1c ISC-1d ISC-1e ISC-1f	ISC-1h ISC-1i ISC-1j ISC-1k ISC-1l	CIP-003-5 R1 - 1.5: Each Responsible Entity, for its high impact and medium impact BES Cyber Systems, shall review and obtain CIP Senior Manager approval at least once every 15 calendar months for one or more documented cyber security policies that collectively address the

Mapping of NIST Cybersecurity Framework v1.0 to NERC CIP version 5 & C2M2 Practices

Function	Category	Subcategory	C2M2 Practices **			NERC CIP v5
			MIL 1	MIL 2	MIL 3	
						following topics: Incident reporting and response planning (CIP-008);
RESPOND (RS)	**Communications (CO):** Response activities are coordinated with internal and external stakeholders, as appropriate, to include external support from law enforcement agencies.	**RS.CO-5:** Voluntary information sharing occurs with external stakeholders to achieve broader cybersecurity situational awareness	ISC-1a ISC-1b IR-3c	ISC-1c ISC-1d ISC-1e ISC-1f	ISC-1h ISC-1i ISC-1j ISC-1k ISC-1l	CIP-003-5 R2 - 2.4: Each Responsible Entity for its assets identified in CIP-002-5, Requirement R1, Part R1.3, shall implement, in a manner that identifies, assesses, and corrects deficiencies, one or more documented cyber security policies that collectively address the following topics, and review and obtain CIP Senior Manager approval for those policies at least once every 15 calendar months: (An inventory, list, or discrete identification of low impact BES Cyber Systems or their BES Cyber Assets is not required). Incident response to a Cyber Security Incident.
RESPOND (RS)	**Communications (CO):** Response activities are coordinated with internal and external stakeholders, as appropriate, to include external support from law enforcement agencies.	**RS.CO-5:** Voluntary information sharing occurs with external stakeholders to achieve broader cybersecurity situational awareness	ISC-1a ISC-1b IR-3c	ISC-1c ISC-1d ISC-1e ISC-1f	ISC-1h ISC-1i ISC-1j ISC-1k ISC-1l	CIP-008-5 R1: Each Responsible Entity shall document one or more Cyber Security Incident response plan(s) that collectively include each of the applicable requirement parts in CIP-008-5 Table R1 – Cyber Security Incident Response Plan Specifications.
RESPOND (RS)	**Communications (CO):** Response activities are coordinated with internal and external stakeholders, as appropriate, to include external support from law enforcement agencies.	**RS.CO-5:** Voluntary information sharing occurs with external stakeholders to achieve broader cybersecurity situational awareness	ISC-1a ISC-1b IR-3c	ISC-1c ISC-1d ISC-1e ISC-1f	ISC-1h ISC-1i ISC-1j ISC-1k ISC-1l	CIP-008-5 R2: Each Responsible Entity shall implement each of its documented Cyber Security Incident response plans to collectively include each of the applicable requirement parts in CIP-008-5 Table R2 – Cyber Security Incident Response Plan Implementation and Testing.

Mapping of NIST Cybersecurity Framework v1.0 to NERC CIP version 5 & C2M2 Practices

Function	Category	Subcategory	C2M2 Practices **			NERC CIP v5
			MIL 1	MIL 2	MIL 3	
RESPOND (RS)	Analysis (AN): Analysis is conducted to ensure adequate response and support recovery activities.	RS.AN-1: Notifications from detection systems are investigated		IR-1e SA-3a	IR-1f IR-1h	CIP-003-5 R1 - 1.5: Each Responsible Entity, for its high impact and medium impact BES Cyber Systems, shall review and obtain CIP Senior Manager approval at least once every 15 calendar months for one or more documented cyber security policies that collectively address the following topics: Incident reporting and response planning (CIP-008);
RESPOND (RS)	Analysis (AN): Analysis is conducted to ensure adequate response and support recovery activities.	RS.AN-1: Notifications from detection systems are investigated		IR-1e SA-3a	IR-1f IR-1h	CIP-003-5 R2 - 2.4: Each Responsible Entity for its assets identified in CIP-002-5, Requirement R1, Part R1.3, shall implement, in a manner that identifies, assesses, and corrects deficiencies, one or more documented cyber security policies that collectively address the following topics, and review and obtain CIP Senior Manager approval for those policies at least once every 15 calendar months: (An inventory, list, or discrete identification of low impact BES Cyber Systems or their BES Cyber Assets is not required). Incident response to a Cyber Security Incident.
RESPOND (RS)	Analysis (AN): Analysis is conducted to ensure adequate response and support recovery activities.	RS.AN-1: Notifications from detection systems are investigated		IR-1e SA-3a	IR-1f IR-1h	CIP-006-5 R1 - 1.5: Issue an alarm or alert in response to detected unauthorized access through a physical access point into a Physical Security Perimeter to the personnel identified in the BES Cyber Security Incident response plan within 15 minutes of detection.
RESPOND (RS)	Analysis (AN): Analysis is conducted to ensure adequate response and support recovery activities.	RS.AN-1: Notifications from detection systems are investigated		IR-1e SA-3a	IR-1f IR-1h	CIP-006-5 R1 - 1.7: Issue an alarm or alert in response to detected unauthorized physical access to a Physical Access Control System to the personnel identified in the BES Cyber

Mapping of NIST Cybersecurity Framework v1.0 to NERC CIP version 5 & C2M2 Practices

Function	Category	Subcategory	C2M2 Practices **			NERC CIP v5
			MIL 1	MIL 2	MIL 3	
						Security Incident response plan within 15 minutes of the detection.
RESPOND (RS)	Analysis (AN): Analysis is conducted to ensure adequate response and support recovery activities.	RS.AN-1: Notifications from detection systems are investigated		IR-1e SA-3a	IR-1f IR-1h	CIP-007-5 R4: Each Responsible Entity shall implement, in a manner that identifies, assesses, and corrects deficiencies, one or more documented processes that collectively include each of the applicable requirement parts in CIP-007-5 Table R4 – Security Event Monitoring.
RESPOND (RS)	Analysis (AN): Analysis is conducted to ensure adequate response and support recovery activities.	RS.AN-1: Notifications from detection systems are investigated		IR-1e SA-3a	IR-1f IR-1h	CIP-008-5 R2: Each Responsible Entity shall implement each of its documented Cyber Security Incident response plans to collectively include each of the applicable requirement parts in CIP-008-5 Table R2 – Cyber Security Incident Response Plan Implementation and Testing.
RESPOND (RS)	Analysis (AN): Analysis is conducted to ensure adequate response and support recovery activities.	RS.AN-2: The impact of the incident is understood	IR-2d IR-2g	IR-2d TVM-1d	IR-2g RM-2j	CIP-008-5 R2: Each Responsible Entity shall implement each of its documented Cyber Security Incident response plans to collectively include each of the applicable requirement parts in CIP-008-5 Table R2 – Cyber Security Incident Response Plan Implementation and Testing.
RESPOND (RS)	Analysis (AN): Analysis is conducted to ensure adequate response and support recovery activities.	RS.AN-3: Forensics are performed		IR-3d	IR-3i	CIP-003-5 R1 - 1.5: Each Responsible Entity, for its high impact and medium impact BES Cyber Systems, shall review and obtain CIP Senior Manager approval at least once every 15 calendar months for one or more documented cyber security policies that collectively address the following topics: Incident reporting and response planning (CIP-008);

Mapping of NIST Cybersecurity Framework v1.0 to NERC CIP version 5 & C2M2 Practices					
			C2M2 Practices **		
Function	Category	Subcategory	MIL 1	MIL 2	MIL 3	NERC CIP v5
RESPOND (RS)	Analysis (AN): Analysis is conducted to ensure adequate response and support recovery activities.	RS.AN-3: Forensics are performed		IR-3d	IR-3i	CIP-008-5 R1: Each Responsible Entity shall document one or more Cyber Security Incident response plan(s) that collectively include each of the applicable requirement parts in CIP-008-5 Table R1 – Cyber Security Incident Response Plan Specifications.
RESPOND (RS)	Analysis (AN): Analysis is conducted to ensure adequate response and support recovery activities.	RS.AN-3: Forensics are performed		IR-3d	IR-3i	CIP-008-5 R2: Each Responsible Entity shall implement each of its documented Cyber Security Incident response plans to collectively include each of the applicable requirement parts in CIP-008-5 Table R2 – Cyber Security Incident Response Plan Implementation and Testing.
RESPOND (RS)	Analysis (AN): Analysis is conducted to ensure adequate response and support recovery activities.	RS.AN-3: Forensics are performed		IR-3d	IR-3i	CIP-009-5 R1 - 1.5: One or more processes to preserve data, per Cyber Asset capability, for determining the cause of a Cyber Security Incident that triggers activation of the recovery plan(s). Data preservation should not impede or restrict recovery.
RESPOND (RS)	Analysis (AN): Analysis is conducted to ensure adequate response and support recovery activities.	RS.AN-4: Incidents are categorized consistent with response plans	IR-2a	IR-1d IR-1e IR-2d TVM-1d	IR-2g RM-1c	CIP-003-5 R1 - 1.5: Each Responsible Entity, for its high impact and medium impact BES Cyber Systems, shall review and obtain CIP Senior Manager approval at least once every 15 calendar months for one or more documented cyber security policies that collectively address the following topics: Incident reporting and response planning (CIP-008);

Mapping of NIST Cybersecurity Framework v1.0 to NERC CIP version 5 & C2M2 Practices

Function	Category	Subcategory	C2M2 Practices **			NERC CIP v5
			MIL 1	MIL 2	MIL 3	
RESPOND (RS)	**Analysis (AN):** Analysis is conducted to ensure adequate response and support recovery activities.	**RS.AN-4:** Incidents are categorized consistent with response plans	IR-2a	IR-1d IR-1e IR-2d TVM-1d	IR-2g RM-1c	CIP-003-5 R2 - 2.4: Each Responsible Entity for its assets identified in CIP-002-5, Requirement R1, Part R1.3, shall implement, in a manner that identifies, assesses, and corrects deficiencies, one or more documented cyber security policies that collectively address the following topics, and review and obtain CIP Senior Manager approval for those policies at least once every 15 calendar months: (An inventory, list, or discrete identification of low impact BES Cyber Systems or their BES Cyber Assets is not required). Incident response to a Cyber Security Incident.
RESPOND (RS)	**Analysis (AN):** Analysis is conducted to ensure adequate response and support recovery activities.	**RS.AN-4:** Incidents are categorized consistent with response plans	IR-2a	IR-1d IR-1e IR-2d TVM-1d	IR-2g RM-1c	CIP-008-5 R1: Each Responsible Entity shall document one or more Cyber Security Incident response plan(s) that collectively include each of the applicable requirement parts in CIP-008-5 Table R1 – Cyber Security Incident Response Plan Specifications.
RESPOND (RS)	**Analysis (AN):** Analysis is conducted to ensure adequate response and support recovery activities.	**RS.AN-4:** Incidents are categorized consistent with response plans	IR-2a	IR-1d IR-1e IR-2d TVM-1d	IR-2g RM-1c	CIP-008-5 R2: Each Responsible Entity shall implement each of its documented Cyber Security Incident response plans to collectively include each of the applicable requirement parts in CIP-008-5 Table R2 – Cyber Security Incident Response Plan Implementation and Testing.
RESPOND (RS)	**Mitigation (MI):** Activities are performed to prevent expansion of an event, mitigate its effects, and eradicate the incident.	**RS.MI-1:** Incidents are contained	IR-3b			CIP-003-5 R1 - 1.5: Each Responsible Entity, for its high impact and medium impact BES Cyber Systems, shall review and obtain CIP Senior Manager approval at least once every 15 calendar months for one or more documented cyber security policies that collectively address the

Mapping of NIST Cybersecurity Framework v1.0 to NERC CIP version 5 & C2M2 Practices

Function	Category	Subcategory	C2M2 Practices **			NERC CIP v5
			MIL 1	MIL 2	MIL 3	
						following topics: Incident reporting and response planning (CIP-008);
RESPOND (RS)	**Mitigation (MI):** Activities are performed to prevent expansion of an event, mitigate its effects, and eradicate the incident.	**RS.MI-1:** Incidents are contained	IR-3b			CIP-003-5 R1 - 1.9: Each Responsible Entity, for its high impact and medium impact BES Cyber Systems, shall review and obtain CIP Senior Manager approval at least once every 15 calendar months for one or more documented cyber security policies that collectively address the following topics: Declaring and responding to CIP Exceptional Circumstances.
RESPOND (RS)	**Mitigation (MI):** Activities are performed to prevent expansion of an event, mitigate its effects, and eradicate the incident.	**RS.MI-1:** Incidents are contained	IR-3b			CIP-003-5 R2 - 2.4: Each Responsible Entity for its assets identified in CIP-002-5, Requirement R1, Part R1.3, shall implement, in a manner that identifies, assesses, and corrects deficiencies, one or more documented cyber security policies that collectively address the following topics, and review and obtain CIP Senior Manager approval for those policies at least once every 15 calendar months: (An inventory, list, or discrete identification of low impact BES Cyber Systems or their BES Cyber Assets is not required). Incident response to a Cyber Security Incident.
RESPOND (RS)	**Mitigation (MI):** Activities are performed to prevent expansion of an event, mitigate its effects, and eradicate the incident.	**RS.MI-1:** Incidents are contained	IR-3b			CIP-005-5 R1 - 1.5: Each Responsible Entity shall implement one or more documented processes that collectively include each of the applicable requirement parts in CIP-005-5 Table R1 – Electronic Security Perimeter. Have one or more

Mapping of NIST Cybersecurity Framework v1.0 to NERC CIP version 5 & C2M2 Practices

Function	Category	Subcategory	C2M2 Practices **			NERC CIP v5
			MIL 1	MIL 2	MIL 3	
						methods for detecting known or suspected malicious communications for both inbound and outbound communications.
RESPOND (RS)	Mitigation (MI): Activities are performed to prevent expansion of an event, mitigate its effects, and eradicate the incident.	RS.MI-1: Incidents are contained	IR-3b			CIP-006-5 R1 - 1.5: Issue an alarm or alert in response to detected unauthorized access through a physical access point into a Physical Security Perimeter to the personnel identified in the BES Cyber Security Incident response plan within 15 minutes of detection.
RESPOND (RS)	Mitigation (MI): Activities are performed to prevent expansion of an event, mitigate its effects, and eradicate the incident.	RS.MI-1: Incidents are contained	IR-3b			CIP-006-5 R1 - 1.7: Issue an alarm or alert in response to detected unauthorized physical access to a Physical Access Control System to the personnel identified in the BES Cyber Security Incident response plan within 15 minutes of the detection.
RESPOND (RS)	Mitigation (MI): Activities are performed to prevent expansion of an event, mitigate its effects, and eradicate the incident.	RS.MI-1: Incidents are contained	IR-3b			CIP-007-5 R3: Each Responsible Entity shall implement, in a manner that identifies, assesses, and corrects deficiencies, one or more documented processes that collectively include each of the applicable requirement parts in CIP-007-5 Table R3 – Malicious Code Prevention.
RESPOND (RS)	Mitigation (MI): Activities are performed to prevent expansion of an event, mitigate its effects, and eradicate the incident.	RS.MI-1: Incidents are contained	IR-3b			CIP-007-5 R4: Each Responsible Entity shall implement, in a manner that identifies, assesses, and corrects deficiencies, one or more documented processes that collectively include each of the applicable requirement parts in CIP-007-5 Table R4 – Security Event Monitoring.

Mapping of NIST Cybersecurity Framework v1.0 to NERC CIP version 5 & C2M2 Practices

Function	Category	Subcategory	C2M2 Practices **			NERC CIP v5
			MIL 1	MIL 2	MIL 3	
RESPOND (RS)	Mitigation (MI): Activities are performed to prevent expansion of an event, mitigate its effects, and eradicate the incident.	RS.MI-1: Incidents are contained	IR-3b			CIP-008-5 R2: Each Responsible Entity shall implement each of its documented Cyber Security Incident response plans to collectively include each of the applicable requirement parts in CIP-008-5 Table R2 – Cyber Security Incident Response Plan Implementation and Testing.
RESPOND (RS)	Mitigation (MI): Activities are performed to prevent expansion of an event, mitigate its effects, and eradicate the incident.	RS.MI-2: Incidents are mitigated	IR-3b			CIP-003-5 R1 - 1.5: Each Responsible Entity, for its high impact and medium impact BES Cyber Systems, shall review and obtain CIP Senior Manager approval at least once every 15 calendar months for one or more documented cyber security policies that collectively address the following topics: Incident reporting and response planning (CIP-008);
RESPOND (RS)	Mitigation (MI): Activities are performed to prevent expansion of an event, mitigate its effects, and eradicate the incident.	RS.MI-2: Incidents are mitigated	IR-3b			CIP-003-5 R1 - 1.9: Each Responsible Entity, for its high impact and medium impact BES Cyber Systems, shall review and obtain CIP Senior Manager approval at least once every 15 calendar months for one or more documented cyber security policies that collectively address the following topics: Declaring and responding to CIP Exceptional Circumstances.
RESPOND (RS)	Mitigation (MI): Activities are performed to prevent expansion of an event, mitigate its effects, and eradicate the incident.	RS.MI-2: Incidents are mitigated	IR-3b			CIP-003-5 R2 - 2.4: Each Responsible Entity for its assets identified in CIP-002-5, Requirement R1, Part R1.3, shall implement, in a manner that identifies, assesses, and corrects deficiencies, one or more documented cyber security policies that collectively address the following topics, and review and obtain CIP Senior Manager approval for those policies at least once every 15 calendar months: (An inventory, list, or discrete identification of low impact BES Cyber

128

Mapping of NIST Cybersecurity Framework v1.0 to NERC CIP version 5 & C2M2 Practices

Function	Category	Subcategory	C2M2 Practices **			NERC CIP v5
			MIL 1	MIL 2	MIL 3	
						Systems or their BES Cyber Assets is not required). Incident response to a Cyber Security Incident.
RESPOND (RS)	Mitigation (MI): Activities are performed to prevent expansion of an event, mitigate its effects, and eradicate the incident.	RS.MI-2: Incidents are mitigated	IR-3b			CIP-005-5 R1 - 1.5: Each Responsible Entity shall implement one or more documented processes that collectively include each of the applicable requirement parts in CIP-005-5 Table R1 – Electronic Security Perimeter. Have one or more methods for detecting known or suspected malicious communications for both inbound and outbound communications.
RESPOND (RS)	Mitigation (MI): Activities are performed to prevent expansion of an event, mitigate its effects, and eradicate the incident.	RS.MI-2: Incidents are mitigated	IR-3b			CIP-006-5 R1 - 1.5: Issue an alarm or alert in response to detected unauthorized access through a physical access point into a Physical Security Perimeter to the personnel identified in the BES Cyber Security Incident response plan within 15 minutes of detection.
RESPOND (RS)	Mitigation (MI): Activities are performed to prevent expansion of an event, mitigate its effects, and eradicate the incident.	RS.MI-2: Incidents are mitigated	IR-3b			CIP-006-5 R1 - 1.7: Issue an alarm or alert in response to detected unauthorized physical access to a Physical Access Control System to the personnel identified in the BES Cyber Security Incident response plan within 15 minutes of the detection.

Mapping of NIST Cybersecurity Framework v1.0 to NERC CIP version 5 & C2M2 Practices

Function	Category	Subcategory	C2M2 Practices **			NERC CIP v5
			MIL 1	MIL 2	MIL 3	
RESPOND (RS)	**Mitigation (MI):** Activities are performed to prevent expansion of an event, mitigate its effects, and eradicate the incident.	**RS.MI-2:** Incidents are mitigated	IR-3b			CIP-007-5 R3: Each Responsible Entity shall implement, in a manner that identifies, assesses, and corrects deficiencies, one or more documented processes that collectively include each of the applicable requirement parts in CIP-007-5 Table R3 – Malicious Code Prevention.
RESPOND (RS)	**Mitigation (MI):** Activities are performed to prevent expansion of an event, mitigate its effects, and eradicate the incident.	**RS.MI-2:** Incidents are mitigated	IR-3b			CIP-007-5 R4: Each Responsible Entity shall implement, in a manner that identifies, assesses, and corrects deficiencies, one or more documented processes that collectively include each of the applicable requirement parts in CIP-007-5 Table R4 – Security Event Monitoring.
RESPOND (RS)	**Mitigation (MI):** Activities are performed to prevent expansion of an event, mitigate its effects, and eradicate the incident.	**RS.MI-2:** Incidents are mitigated	IR-3b			CIP-008-5 R2: Each Responsible Entity shall implement each of its documented Cyber Security Incident response plans to collectively include each of the applicable requirement parts in CIP-008-5 Table R2 – Cyber Security Incident Response Plan Implementation and Testing.
RESPOND (RS)	**Mitigation (MI):** Activities are performed to prevent expansion of an event, mitigate its effects, and eradicate the incident.	**RS.MI-3:** Newly identified vulnerabilities are mitigated or documented as accepted risks	TVM-2c	TVM-2f TVM-2g	RM-2j TVM-2m TVM-2n	CIP-003-5 R1 - 1.7: Each Responsible Entity, for its high impact and medium impact BES Cyber Systems, shall review and obtain CIP Senior Manager approval at least once every 15 calendar months for one or more documented cyber security policies that collectively address the following topics: Configuration change management and vulnerability assessments (CIP-010);

Mapping of NIST Cybersecurity Framework v1.0 to NERC CIP version 5 & C2M2 Practices

Function	Category	Subcategory	C2M2 Practices **			NERC CIP v5
			MIL 1	MIL 2	MIL 3	
RESPOND (RS)	**Mitigation (MI):** Activities are performed to prevent expansion of an event, mitigate its effects, and eradicate the incident.	**RS.MI-3:** Newly identified vulnerabilities are mitigated or documented as accepted risks	TVM-2c	TVM-2f TVM-2g	RM-2j TVM-2m TVM-2n	CIP-007-5 R2: Each Responsible Entity shall implement, in a manner that identifies, assesses, and corrects deficiencies, one or more documented processes that collectively include each of the applicable requirement parts in CIP-007-5 Table R2 – Security Patch Management.
RESPOND (RS)	**Mitigation (MI):** Activities are performed to prevent expansion of an event, mitigate its effects, and eradicate the incident.	**RS.MI-3:** Newly identified vulnerabilities are mitigated or documented as accepted risks	TVM-2c	TVM-2f TVM-2g	RM-2j TVM-2m TVM-2n	CIP-007-5 R3: Each Responsible Entity shall implement, in a manner that identifies, assesses, and corrects deficiencies, one or more documented processes that collectively include each of the applicable requirement parts in CIP-007-5 Table R3 – Malicious Code Prevention.
RESPOND (RS)	**Mitigation (MI):** Activities are performed to prevent expansion of an event, mitigate its effects, and eradicate the incident.	**RS.MI-3:** Newly identified vulnerabilities are mitigated or documented as accepted risks	TVM-2c	TVM-2f TVM-2g	RM-2j TVM-2m TVM-2n	CIP-010-1 R3: Each Responsible Entity shall implement one or more documented processes that collectively include each of the applicable requirement parts in CIP-010 - 1 Table R3– Vulnerability Assessments.
RESPOND (RS)	**Improvements (IM):** Organizational response activities are improved by incorporating lessons learned from current and previous detection/response activities.	**RS.IM-1:** Response plans incorporate lessons learned			IR-3h	CIP-003-5 R1 - 1.5: Each Responsible Entity, for its high impact and medium impact BES Cyber Systems, shall review and obtain CIP Senior Manager approval at least once every 15 calendar months for one or more documented cyber security policies that collectively address the following topics: Incident reporting and response planning (CIP-008);

Mapping of NIST Cybersecurity Framework v1.0 to NERC CIP version 5 & C2M2 Practices

Function	Category	Subcategory	C2M2 Practices **			NERC CIP v5
			MIL 1	MIL 2	MIL 3	
RESPOND (RS)	**Improvements (IM):** Organizational response activities are improved by incorporating lessons learned from current and previous detection/response activities.	**RS.IM-1:** Response plans incorporate lessons learned			IR-3h	CIP-003-5 R2 - 2.4: Each Responsible Entity for its assets identified in CIP-002-5, Requirement R1, Part R1.3, shall implement, in a manner that identifies, assesses, and corrects deficiencies, one or more documented cyber security policies that collectively address the following topics, and review and obtain CIP Senior Manager approval for those policies at least once every 15 calendar months: (An inventory, list, or discrete identification of low impact BES Cyber Systems or their BES Cyber Assets is not required). Incident response to a Cyber Security Incident.
RESPOND (RS)	**Improvements (IM):** Organizational response activities are improved by incorporating lessons learned from current and previous detection/response activities.	**RS.IM-1:** Response plans incorporate lessons learned			IR-3h	CIP-008-5 R2: Each Responsible Entity shall implement each of its documented Cyber Security Incident response plans to collectively include each of the applicable requirement parts in CIP-008-5 Table R2 – Cyber Security Incident Response Plan Implementation and Testing.
RESPOND (RS)	**Improvements (IM):** Organizational response activities are improved by incorporating lessons learned from current and previous detection/response activities.	**RS.IM-1:** Response plans incorporate lessons learned			IR-3h	CIP-008-5 R3: Each Responsible Entity shall maintain each of its Cyber Security Incident response plans according to each of the applicable requirement parts in CIP-008-5 Table R3 – Cyber Security Incident Response Plan Review, Update, and Communication.
RESPOND (RS)	**Improvements (IM):** Organizational response activities are improved by incorporating lessons learned from current and previous detection/response activities.	**RS.IM-2:** Response strategies are updated	IR-3e		IR-3k	CIP-003-5 R1 - 1.5: Each Responsible Entity, for its high impact and medium impact BES Cyber Systems, shall review and obtain CIP Senior Manager approval at least once every 15 calendar months for one or more documented cyber security policies that collectively address the

Mapping of NIST Cybersecurity Framework v1.0 to NERC CIP version 5 & C2M2 Practices

Function	Category	Subcategory	C2M2 Practices **			NERC CIP v5
			MIL 1	MIL 2	MIL 3	
						following topics: Incident reporting and response planning (CIP-008);
RESPOND (RS)	**Improvements (IM):** Organizational response activities are improved by incorporating lessons learned from current and previous detection/response activities.	**RS.IM-2:** Response strategies are updated	IR-3e		IR-3k	CIP-003-5 R2 - 2.4: Each Responsible Entity for its assets identified in CIP-002-5, Requirement R1, Part R1.3, shall implement, in a manner that identifies, assesses, and corrects deficiencies, one or more documented cyber security policies that collectively address the following topics, and review and obtain CIP Senior Manager approval for those policies at least once every 15 calendar months: (An inventory, list, or discrete identification of low impact BES Cyber Systems or their BES Cyber Assets is not required). Incident response to a Cyber Security Incident.
RESPOND (RS)	**Improvements (IM):** Organizational response activities are improved by incorporating lessons learned from current and previous detection/response activities.	**RS.IM-2:** Response strategies are updated	IR-3e		IR-3k	CIP-008-5 R1: Each Responsible Entity shall document one or more Cyber Security Incident response plan(s) that collectively include each of the applicable requirement parts in CIP-008-5 Table R1 – Cyber Security Incident Response Plan Specifications.
RESPOND (RS)	**Improvements (IM):** Organizational response activities are improved by incorporating lessons learned from current and previous detection/response activities.	**RS.IM-2:** Response strategies are updated	IR-3e		IR-3k	CIP-008-5 R2: Each Responsible Entity shall implement each of its documented Cyber Security Incident response plans to collectively include each of the applicable requirement parts in CIP-008-5 Table R2 – Cyber Security Incident Response Plan Implementation and Testing.

Mapping of NIST Cybersecurity Framework v1.0 to NERC CIP version 5 & C2M2 Practices						
Function	Category	Subcategory	C2M2 Practices **			NERC CIP v5
			MIL 1	MIL 2	MIL 3	
RESPOND (RS)	**Improvements (IM):** Organizational response activities are improved by incorporating lessons learned from current and previous detection/response activities.	**RS.IM-2:** Response strategies are updated	IR-3e		IR-3k	CIP-008-5 R3: Each Responsible Entity shall maintain each of its Cyber Security Incident response plans according to each of the applicable requirement parts in CIP-008-5 Table R3 – Cyber Security Incident Response Plan Review, Update, and Communication.
RECOVER (RC)	**Recovery Planning (RP):** Recovery processes and procedures are executed and maintained to ensure timely restoration of systems or assets affected by cybersecurity events.	**RC.RP-1:** Recovery plan is executed during or after an event	IR-3b		IR-3o IR-4k	CIP-003-5 R1 - 1.5: Each Responsible Entity, for its high impact and medium impact BES Cyber Systems, shall review and obtain CIP Senior Manager approval at least once every 15 calendar months for one or more documented cyber security policies that collectively address the following topics: Incident reporting and response planning (CIP-008);
RECOVER (RC)	**Recovery Planning (RP):** Recovery processes and procedures are executed and maintained to ensure timely restoration of systems or assets affected by cybersecurity events.	**RC.RP-1:** Recovery plan is executed during or after an event	IR-3b		IR-3o IR-4k	CIP-003-5 R1 - 1.6: Each Responsible Entity, for its high impact and medium impact BES Cyber Systems, shall review and obtain CIP Senior Manager approval at least once every 15 calendar months for one or more documented cyber security policies that collectively address the following topics: Recovery plans for BES Cyber Systems (CIP-009);
RECOVER (RC)	**Recovery Planning (RP):** Recovery processes and procedures are executed and maintained to ensure timely restoration of systems or assets affected by cybersecurity events.	**RC.RP-1:** Recovery plan is executed during or after an event	IR-3b		IR-3o IR-4k	CIP-007-5 R4: Each Responsible Entity shall implement, in a manner that identifies, assesses, and corrects deficiencies, one or more documented processes that collectively include each of the applicable requirement parts in CIP-007-5 Table R4 – Security Event Monitoring.

134

Mapping of NIST Cybersecurity Framework v1.0 to NERC CIP version 5 & C2M2 Practices

Function	Category	Subcategory	C2M2 Practices **			NERC CIP v5
			MIL 1	MIL 2	MIL 3	
RECOVER (RC)	**Recovery Planning (RP):** Recovery processes and procedures are executed and maintained to ensure timely restoration of systems or assets affected by cybersecurity events.	**RC.RP-1:** Recovery plan is executed during or after an event	IR-3b		IR-3o IR-4k	CIP-009-5 R1: Each Responsible Entity shall have one or more documented recovery plans that collectively include each of the applicable requirement parts in CIP-009-5 Table R1 – Recovery Plan Specifications.
RECOVER (RC)	**Recovery Planning (RP):** Recovery processes and procedures are executed and maintained to ensure timely restoration of systems or assets affected by cybersecurity events.	**RC.RP-1:** Recovery plan is executed during or after an event	IR-3b		IR-3o IR-4k	CIP-009-5 R2: Each Responsible Entity shall implement, in a manner that identifies, assesses, and corrects deficiencies, its documented recovery plan(s) to collectively include each of the applicable requirement parts in CIP-009-5 Table R2 – Recovery Plan Implementation and Testing
RECOVER (RC)	**Recovery Planning (RP):** Recovery processes and procedures are executed and maintained to ensure timely restoration of systems or assets affected by cybersecurity events.	**RC.RP-1:** Recovery plan is executed during or after an event	IR-3b		IR-3o IR-4k	CIP-009-5 R3: Each Responsible Entity shall maintain each of its recovery plans in accordance with each of the applicable requirement parts in CIP-009-5 Table R3 – Recovery Plan Review, Update and Communication.
RECOVER (RC)	**Improvements (IM):** Improvements (IM): Recovery planning and processes are improved by incorporating lessons learned into future activities.	**RC.IM-1:** Recovery plans incorporate lessons learned			IR-3h IR-4i IR-3k	CIP-003-5 R1 - 1.6: Each Responsible Entity, for its high impact and medium impact BES Cyber Systems, shall review and obtain CIP Senior Manager approval at least once every 15 calendar months for one or more documented cyber security policies that collectively address the following topics: Recovery plans for BES Cyber Systems (CIP-009);
RECOVER (RC)	**Improvements (IM):** Improvements (IM): Recovery planning and processes are improved by incorporating lessons learned into future activities.	**RC.IM-1:** Recovery plans incorporate lessons learned			IR-3h IR-4i IR-3k	CIP-009-5 R3: Each Responsible Entity shall maintain each of its recovery plans in accordance with each of the applicable requirement parts in CIP-009-5 Table R3 – Recovery Plan Review, Update and Communication.

Mapping of NIST Cybersecurity Framework v1.0 to NERC CIP version 5 & C2M2 Practices

Function	Category	Subcategory	C2M2 Practices **			NERC CIP v5
			MIL 1	MIL 2	MIL 3	
RECOVER (RC)	Improvements (IM): Improvements (IM): Recovery planning and processes are improved by incorporating lessons learned into future activities.	RC.IM-2: Recovery strategies are updated			IR-3h IR-3k	CIP-003-5 R1 - 1.6: Each Responsible Entity, for its high impact and medium impact BES Cyber Systems, shall review and obtain CIP Senior Manager approval at least once every 15 calendar months for one or more documented cyber security policies that collectively address the following topics: Recovery plans for BES Cyber Systems (CIP-009);
RECOVER (RC)	Improvements (IM): Improvements (IM): Recovery planning and processes are improved by incorporating lessons learned into future activities.	RC.IM-2: Recovery strategies are updated			IR-3h IR-3k	CIP-009-5 R3: Each Responsible Entity shall maintain each of its recovery plans in accordance with each of the applicable requirement parts in CIP-009-5 Table R3 – Recovery Plan Review, Update and Communication.
RECOVER (RC)	Communications (CO): Restoration activities are coordinated with internal and external parties, such as coordinating centers, Internet Service Providers, owners of attacking systems, victims, other CSIRTs, and vendors.	RC.CO-1: Public Relations are managed		TVM-1d IR-4d	RM-1c	
RECOVER (RC)	Communications (CO): Restoration activities are coordinated with internal and external parties, such as coordinating centers, Internet Service Providers, owners of attacking systems, victims, other CSIRTs, and vendors.	RC.CO-2: Reputation after an event is repaired		IR-4d		

Mapping of NIST Cybersecurity Framework v1.0 to NERC CIP version 5 & C2M2 Practices

Function	Category	Subcategory	C2M2 Practices **			NERC CIP v5
			MIL 1	MIL 2	MIL 3	
RECOVER (RC)	**Communications (CO):** Restoration activities are coordinated with internal and external parties, such as coordinating centers, Internet Service Providers, owners of attacking systems, victims, other CSIRTs, and vendors.	**RC.CO-3:** Recovery activities are communicated to internal stakeholders and executive and management teams		IR-3d	IR-5e	CIP-003-5 R1 - 1.6: Each Responsible Entity, for its high impact and medium impact BES Cyber Systems, shall review and obtain CIP Senior Manager approval at least once every 15 calendar months for one or more documented cyber security policies that collectively address the following topics: Recovery plans for BES Cyber Systems (CIP-009);
RECOVER (RC)	**Communications (CO):** Restoration activities are coordinated with internal and external parties, such as coordinating centers, Internet Service Providers, owners of attacking systems, victims, other CSIRTs, and vendors.	**RC.CO-3:** Recovery activities are communicated to internal stakeholders and executive and management teams		IR-3d	IR-5e	CIP-009-5 R1: Each Responsible Entity shall have one or more documented recovery plans that collectively include each of the applicable requirement parts in CIP-009-5 Table R1 – Recovery Plan Specifications.
RECOVER (RC)	**Communications (CO):** Restoration activities are coordinated with internal and external parties, such as coordinating centers, Internet Service Providers, owners of attacking systems, victims, other CSIRTs, and vendors.	**RC.CO-3:** Recovery activities are communicated to internal stakeholders and executive and management teams		IR-3d	IR-5e	CIP-009-5 R2: Each Responsible Entity shall implement, in a manner that identifies, assesses, and corrects deficiencies, its documented recovery plan(s) to collectively include each of the applicable requirement parts in CIP-009-5 Table R2 – Recovery Plan Implementation and Testing.
RECOVER (RC)	**Communications (CO):** Restoration activities are coordinated with internal and external parties, such as coordinating centers, Internet Service Providers, owners of attacking systems, victims, other CSIRTs, and vendors.	**RC.CO-3:** Recovery activities are communicated to internal stakeholders and executive and management teams		IR-3d	IR-5e	CIP-009-5 R3: Each Responsible Entity shall maintain each of its recovery plans in accordance with each of the applicable requirement parts in CIP-009-5 Table R3 – Recovery Plan Review, Update and Communication.